HYDROPONICS GROWING SYSTEM

Discover the secret for growing vegetables and fruits in your garden with exclusive hydroponics techniques for a great gardening experience even if you are a beginner

ANDREA M. WILSON

Copyright © 2020 by *Andrea M. Wilson*

- ALL RIGHTS RESERVED -

The content contained within this book may not be reproduced, duplicated or transmitted without direct written permission from the author or the publisher.

Under no circumstances will any blame or legal responsibility be held against the publisher, or author, for any damages, reparation, or monetary loss due to the information contained within this book. either directly or indirectly.

Legal notice:

This book is copyright protected. This book is only for personal use. You cannot amend, distribute, sell, use, quote or paraphrase any part, or the content within this book, without the consent of the author or publisher.

Disclaimer notice:

Please note the information contained within this document is for educational and entertainment purposes only. All effort has been executed to present accurate, up to date, and reliable, complete information. No warranties of any kind are declared or implied. readers acknowledge that the author is not engaging in the rendering of legal , financial, medical or professional advice. the content within this book has been derived from various sources. please consult a licensed professional before attempting any techniques outlined in this book.

By reading this document, the reader agrees that under no circumsta nces is the author responsible for any losses, direct or indirect, which are incurred as a result of the use of the information contained within this document, including, but not limited to, errors, omissions, or inaccuracies.

Table of Contents

Introduction 1

Chapter 1: Is Hydroponics Worth The While? 5

Why Hydroponics? 6

How Plants Grow 7

The Objective Of Hydroponics 9

Pros And Cons Of Hydroponic System 10

Chapter 2: Advantages And Disadvantage 15

Advantages Of A Hydroponic System 15

Disadvantages 19

The Benefits Of Hydroponics 21

Chapter 3: Different Type of Hydroponic Systems 25

The Drip System or Continuous Drip 25

The Ebb and Flow System 27

The water Culture Growing System 29

The Wick System 33

The Aeroponic System 37

The Aquaponic System 37

NFT (Nutrient Film Technique) System 39

Now that you know what 40

Wick System 40

Water Culture System 42

Ebb-Flow System 43

Drip System 45

Nft (Nutrient Film Technique) System 47

Aeroponics System 49

Chapter 4: Choosing The Right Site For Your Garden 53

Humidity 53

Ventilation 55

Carbon Dioxide 56

The Optimal Temperature In Hydroponics 57

Where To Place The Hydroponic Installation? 60

Chapter 5: Assembling The System 61

Wick System 61

Water Culture System 62

Ebb And Flow System 64

Drip System 65

Nutrient Film Technique 66

Aeroponics 67

Chapter 6: Nutrition For Hydroponic Plants 69

Nutrients 69

Nutrient Solution 72

Ph Importance..*75*

Chapter 7: Water Maintenance, Garden Expansion..................79

Water Maintenance...*79*

Garden Expansion...*81*

Important Maintenance Tips..*85*

Adding Nutrients...*88*

Chapter 8: Plant Stages..91

The Rooting Stage...*91*

The Vegetative Stage...*93*

The Flowering Stage..*94*

Chapter 9: Ideal PH Level For Your Hydroponics Plants...........96

What Is PH?..*97*

Testing The PH...*102*

Chapter 10: Water: Quenching Plants' Thirst And Oxygen.......104

Water: Quenching Plants' Thirst..*104*

Oxygen Is Needed To Grow Healthy Vegetables:........................*108*

Chapter 11: Greenhouse Operation..110

Environmental Controls..*112*

Temperature Control...*114*

Selecting A Good Indoor Growing Space & Setting Up..............*118*

Chapter 12: Extra: Other Important Aspects Of A Hydroponics System..120

   Water Level..120

   Lighting...124

   Nutrient Solution Temperature...127

Chapter 13: Some Problems You Might Encounter...................131

   Rust-Like Spots On The Leaves Of Crops............................131

   Treatment: Switch Nutrient Solution...................................132

   Leaves Are Yellowing And Wilting..133

   White Spots On The Leaves...134

   Plants Are Too Big For The System......................................135

   Leaves Appear As If Tips Are Burned..................................136

   Leaves Curling Over...137

   Leaves Curling Under...137

   Leaves Wilting...138

   Leaves Turn Into Purple Toward End Of Flowering Stage.................138

   Flowers Rot..139

   Plants Turning Yellow And Looking Sick...........................139

   Flower Offshoots..140

   Temperature Around The Hydroponic System Is Too High.................140

   Yield Is Smaller Than Usual..141

   White Slime In The Reservoir...142

Chapter 14: Growing Tips And Tricks 143

What Type Of Plants To Grow 143

Solutions To Hydroponic Issues 146

Extra Growing Tips 148

Chapter 15: Business Tips And Information About Hydroponics 150

Conclusion 158

Introduction

Comprehensive studies have been conducted on hydroponic gardening since Gericke. Gericke proved that plants grown in hydroponics systems will grow up to 50% faster than plants grown in soil, as well as growing bigger and healthier fruits, vegetables and herbs. Benefits are not solely related to growth. There are also environmental benefits.

Growth Benefits

- No Yard Required
- Nutrients
- Water-Saving
- Higher Yields
- Affordable
- Enjoyment
- Year-round Growing
- Relaxation
- Family Experience

You do not need a yard to start your hydroponic garden. You can get it set up on a patio, small yard, or in your home, without worries. The nutrients are supplied via the water solution, so you won't have to worry about what plant food to purchase and add to the soil.

Water-saving is often the one thing that puzzles individuals. How can you save water, if you are using a water based gardening system? Think about how you water your plants that are in soil. You are not sure how much to water them or whether there is too much water in the lower layers of soil. There can also be a lot of waste, when the water runs off. With a hydroponic system everything is cycled in containers, so the water goes into the plant container, out the bottom, and into a gray water tank, where the water is then cleaned and cycled around again.

With more nutrients reaching the plant roots through the water, you have higher yields than the one or two fruits/vegetables that grow on your soil based plants.

The initial system can be set up for as little as $50 or as much as $500. It all depends on if you go with pre-made items or build your own hydroponics system. It makes it more affordable than constantly buying new plants, soil, and plant food for a soil based system.

Anyone who grows via hydroponics finds they enjoy gardening more, are relaxed, and can make it a family experience. Designing and setting up the system can involve the entire family. Your children can enjoy picking vegetables, herbs, and fruits right from the plants when they want to eat something.

You also obtain better quality food from your hydroponic garden. It is higher quality because you do not have to worry, as much about pests. There are various ways you can ensure pests do not get into your plants.

Lastly, with a hydroponic garden, you never have to be concerned about frost and frozen ground. You are able to grow your plants indoors or move the system indoors during the colder months. With a year-round yield, you get to eat your favorite fruits and veggies all the time.

Environmental Benefits of Hydroponics

Hydroponics is based on a recycling system. Not only can you recycle the materials you build your system out of, but you can also recycle the water you use. With the recycling system, you are going to use 10% less than many of the traditional hydroponic systems, and definitely 10% less than your regular soil garden.

Pesticides and herbicides that usually flow into the ground as you spray to protect your plants are unneeded with hydroponic gardens, which also benefits the earth. Since you are not dependent on the small slices are earth left with any nutrients to grow your garden, you are also helping the earth with your gardening system.

Soil Garden Benefits

Soil gardens do offer a few benefits. The first is a lower initial cost. You can start your garden with plants in the ground. However, water, fertilizer, and pesticides quickly increase the long term costs of soil gardens.

Soil gardens do not require electricity, and hydroponics gardens will. Most hydroponics gardens are set up indoors and require a proper light source. Some systems also contain electrical pumps to help aerate the water for the roots.

Soil gardening has a lower risk of bacteria and mold growth. Water gardens are moister, which some plants are susceptible to growth mold and bacteria.

Chapter 1

Is hydroponics worth the while?

Gardeners enjoy hydroponics because it's possible to grow almost anything, and there's little or no backbreaking work: no tilling, raking or hoeing. There are no pulling of weeds and no spraying of toxic pesticides. Few moles or cutworms consume the roots, and most insects leave their plants clean and healthy alone.

Hydroponics is suitable for the homeowner or tenant hobbyists who have no time or space for full-time gardening of the land. In late spring and summer, you can place your portable hydroponic unit outside on a porch or balcony where natural sunlight helps to produce tremendous yields from lettuce, to cucumbers, to zinnias. The unit can be moved anywhere inside the home in winter, even into the basement, where your plants will thrive and continue to be produced under artificial light.

Plants love to grow through hydroponics because their roots don't have to pass through thick, chunky soil to fight for nutrients. Alternatively, one hydroponic system equally distributes nutrients to each vine. Plants also need oxygen to breathe, and a porous expanding aggregate, unlike dirt, allows air to circulate around them freely. And everything is growing fast and beautifully.

Hydroponic plants grow quicker, mature earlier and give up the yield of soil-grown plants by up to ten times. This washed and pampered plants produce high nutritional value fruits and vegetables, with outstanding flavor. Many of them, particularly hydroponic tomatoes and cucumbers, are sold at far higher prices than ordinary vegetables in the gourmet sections of supermarkets. The point here is that the same vegetables can be grown for considerably less money than the pulpy supermarket variety costs to buy.

Why hydroponics?

Have you noticed lately that vegetables in supermarkets are missing something? It's all flavor. As with many industrial foods, the taste was substituted for consumer convenience. Large-scale farming and marketing do, of course, provide the world's burgeoning population with vast quantities of food, but it is important to remember that quality suffers whenever quantity is stressed. As a result, your meals ' flavor and nutritional value are reduced.

The varieties of seeds produced for "agribusiness" are one major reason for these declines. These seeds are selected for fast growth and high yield. The resulting vegetables and fruits have rugged skins for processing, storage, and shipping devices. Flavor and price are concerns secondary. Also, many vegetables are harvested unripe, particularly tomatoes, to ensure safe shipment and longer shelf life in the market. In fact, attempts are now being made to develop a hybrid square tomato that fits in packages.

More often than not, cities and villages grew up in frontier days, where farmers till the soil. They were good farmers and had the best soil to choose from. These towns and villages are our present-day cities, still expanding and still engulfing valuable agricultural land. As prime agricultural land disappears, as the costs of growers continue to rise, as transport costs increase in parallel with energy supplies, and as supermarket boards of directors become increasingly concerned with profit margins, we will see our food costs rise to the point of absurdity. World War II's Victory Gardens have been planted to raise unavailable food, and it seems realistic to say millions of people will use hydroponics in the near future to supply themselves with affordable vegetables and herbs of a quality that stores cannot match.

How plants grow

Many hydroponics books, complete with illustrations, give the reader a crash course on plant biology. Relating biology specifically to the hydroponics and the nutrients that help plants grow seems to make more sense.

The growing plant is a natural workshop which constructs organic matter in the form of roots, stems, leaves, fruit, and seed. Less than ninety-seven percent of this matter is provided by air and water, while the rest comes from plant nutrients. No organic substance can be taken up by a plant; instead, it absorbs inorganic mineral salts. That is, the vegetable kingdom feeds directly upon the kingdom of minerals.

There is no dispute, however, between organic gardening and hydroponics. In organic gardening, however, the difference is that it is the soil that is fed with dead plant and animal matter, not the plant. Soil acts as a natural fertilizer factory that works with its soil bacteria in league with weathering to operate on those organic substances. It breaks down these substances into their inorganic composites (chemicals, if you like), so they can be fed upon by the plants.

There is no soil in hydroponics, and the plants are fed directly with the same minerals to produce healthy organic soil. The plant doesn't know if its mineral food was made by man or nature or a particular care pattern. However, it does care that it is well fed, and a nitrate is a nitrate, whether it comes from a solution to the nutrient or a dead mouse.

To grow, a plant utilizes two basic processes. The first, osmosis takes over the roots from water and minerals. The second, photosynthesis, turns the water and minerals into plant tissue using light and the environment. To breathe, roots also need oxygen, and this is one of the reasons that hydroponics functions so well. The loose, chunky growing medium hydroponic, the aggregate, as it's called, allows plenty of air to reach the roots. Natural soil, on the other hand, often requires much work and time to ensure satisfactory aeration.

Plants mainly grow with the help of a process called photosynthesis. They use sunlight and chlorophyll to convert water and carbon dioxide into oxygen and glucose. There's no implicit or explicit mention of soil anywhere in the process and therefore, it could be concluded that plants only need nutrients and water to survive. Water and nutrients can easily be obtained from soil or any other source or medium.

Hydroponics is a process by which plants are grown without using any soil. The procedure involves the use of a water solvent along with a mineral nutrient solution, which aids in the efficient intake of various nutrients by the plant. This whole process is a subset of hydroculture.

The objective of hydroponics

The main objective of hydroponics is to provide the ideal environment for the plants through which they can obtain the required nutrition essential for their sustenance. Climate and lighting can also be controlled to improve the yield of plants, including a greenhouse set up with natural and supplemental lighting.

The science behind hydroponics

The backbone of hydroponics depends on the discovery of basic nutrients needed for a plant to survive and also the way of processing the said nutrients. It has helped scientists to develop hydroponic solutions that will optimize the development of specific plants during their growth timeline. For example, nitrogen is used by plants during the young growth phase, while phosphorus is used during the blooming stage (fruits and flowers).

The advantages of hydroponics

• Due to the intake of a perfectly balanced diet, plants grown hydroponically are much healthier than their counterparts grown on soil.

• There is no use of herbicides and pesticides in the hydroponic process. Thus, the cost of chemicals and labor are reduced.

• Hydroponically grown plants provide higher yields and can be grown closely together without one affecting the growth of the other.

• Conditions like drought or floods do not affect the hydroponic system. Hydroponically plants can be grown in areas where water is scarce. Also, there's no soil runoff and evaporation is prevented.

Pros and cons of hydroponic system

The hydroponic system is excellent because it is easy to build and less expensive to make. It can also be maintained comfortably, once after you have set it up. You can also scale its setup hassle-free from growing a few plants for your home to a bunch of the whole crops if you wish to sell your grown products in the market. The significant need of an hour for the entire world is to save water, and hydroponics support this cause. It saves more than 90% of the water if we compare this farming with soil farming.

The major drawback of the hydroponics over the soil is that it is a bit complex as compared to soil farming and requires intensive care for growth management. You need in-depth experience and knowledge throughout the process of the plant's growth.

Once you have developed your expertise and skills into hydroponics, it will provide you better results at a lower cost.

Nutrients for hydroponics

Hydroponic nutrients could be a complex issue or as simple as pouring and mixing. The people who are new to hydroponics and are not familiar with the fertigation techniques, follow the template on the medicine. It will make you learn how to use the nutrients to provide it to the plants.

So the main questions about hydroponic nutrients when you are a beginner could be choosing your fertilizer? What nutrients should you add? How often and how much you have provided nutrients to your plants?

Let us first find out how to choose your fertilizer. Mixing hydroponic nutrients can surely be a breeze. When you are about to select your fertilizer, there are two deciding factors, i.e., wet vs. dry. Also, what plants are you growing inside that set up is essential, based on which you need to disperse the nutrients to all plants. Different nutrients are required for different plants. If you are growing commercially, dry fertilizers will be appropriate for you.

The nutrients like NPK (Nitrogen, Phosphorous, and Potassium) which are known to be macronutrients are required by almost every type of plant. NPK comes in dozens of different ratios as plants with distinctive properties, and variety requires different proportions of NPK and other micronutrients. For example- Capsicum requires more calcium, while Cucumber requires magnesium in larger quantity.

What nutrients should be added?

Different mixes will give you a different product altogether. For example 13 0 45 (NPK) has 13% of nitrogen, no phosphorus, and 45% of potassium, which makes this product called potassium nitrate. Whereas, 0 0 50 (NPK) has no nitrogen, no phosphorus, 50% of potassium, and this product is called as Potassium sulfate.

Usually, for hydroponic use, you need four nutrients mixed regularly to fertilize your plants. These are-

1) NPK mix (Of different types depending upon the plant)

2) Magnesium sulfate

3) Calcium Nitrate

4) Sulfur

5) Other micronutrients solution (If needed such as iron, zinc, copper, manganese, etc.)

Your plants will claim Oxygen, Carbon, and hydrogen from the air and water around them. The rest, you will be using in your nutrient mix, including NPK, calcium, magnesium, sulfur, and other micronutrients fertilizer which is readily available in the market.

How much and how often you should provide nutrients to the plants?

You need to check the label on the nutrient mix and follow that instruction to check how much you ought to provide that specific nutrient to the plants. For example- while you are giving magnesium sulfate, you need to check the label for ensuring the appropriate dosage required per plant.

You need to make sure what is your nutrient level of the plant before giving any nutrient mix. Top off your systems after a few days at a fixed interval and then disperse nutrients to compensate for both the dilution of the top off and the plant use.

Chapter 2

Advantages and disadvantage

Advantages of a hydroponic system

1) No need for soil

It is one of the biggest and sole reasons why people are moving towards hydroponic farming or gardening. In the 1940s, the first initiative or we can say a successful experiment was done on hydroponic when some vegetables were grown for the troops. On the other hand, we can use this method where the soil is no longer suitable for farming and plant growth.

Hydroponic is considered as the most preferred way for growing vegetables in space for astronauts in the future, NASA stated.

2) Greater use of space

It is another drastic benefit of hydroponic because you need to install a hydroponic system in your house or a place. It requires less space and can fit in any location. Whether you want to establish your hydroponic system in your apartment or farmhouse, it's totally up to you.

The plant roots are usually spread to get the essential nutrients from the soil, but this technique will provide all the necessary elements within a reservoir.

3) Climate control

Indeed, a hydroponic grower has total control over the climate condition to grow something in the hydroponic system. The reason is when we do traditional farming or vegetable growing; then we need to work according to the climate and seasons. But here, you have all the total control over the environment, seasons, light intensification, temperature, humidity, and air composition.

It means you can grow anything without facing the difficulties of weather and climate and earn a lot of money.

4) Water-saving technique

After meeting the significant crises of water in various parts of the world, the proper and efficient use of water has now become the burning issue of debates. The ground level of water is mitigating day by day, and a recent study says that around 80 percent of ground and surface water is consumed through agriculture in America.

Hydroponic is the best way to preserve the water level because it requires only 10 percent of water in comparison to soil-based farming. Through this way, we can save a tremendous amount of water and can grow healthy crops.

5) Better use of nutrients

It is another great benefit of doing hydroponic based farming because through this technique, we use nutrients most effectively. It means we can accurately use the needed nutrients to grow the plant. By mixing essential nutrients solutions with water to grow the plants, we can save the loss of nutrients.

6) Solution- PH control

Through the hydroponic system, we can contain all the minerals and nutrients solutions in the water. And that solely means we can also adjust or measure the PH levels of water mixture in comparison to soil-based farming. And this ensures the desirable consumption of nutrients for the plant.

7) Healthy growth rate

Indeed, you can grow more-faster and healthier plants through hydroponics. The logic is elementary because when you have the total command over something, then the results will also come in your favor. Through hydroponics, you can control the level of PH, mix needed nutrients solutions, add required water, use of a scientific method, better control over climate, temperature and air intensification, and all these aspects can give you the most desired results.

8) No weeds

The relation of weeds with soil-based farming and gardening is one of the frustrating relationships the world has ever seen. And the task of weed elimination from the garden is also time-consuming. The more you cut them, the more they will grow. So, it is better to avoid the idea of soil-based farming or gardening and opt for the hydroponic method.

9) Fewer diseases

By selecting the mode of hydroponic, you can be able to avoid the frustrating issues like weeds, plant destructive pests like gophers, birds, groundhogs, and some soul-based diseases like Pythium, Fusarium and Rhizoctonia species. By doing hydroponic farming, you can avoid all these time taking and harming issues.

10) Lesser use of herbicides and insecticides

The heavy use of herbicides and pesticides to remove or eradicate the diseases, pests, weeds, and other unwanted things from soil to prevent the plant makes the plant unhealthy and chemically infected. Buy avoiding the land-based growing you can grow more-cleaner and healthier plants.

11) Time and labor saver

Farming is the most-simplest yet arduous work in the world. You need to devote your healthy amount of time to produce or grow desired plants. The process of watering, cultivation, tilling, and eradication of pests and weeds require a significant amount of time. So, if you want to get desired results in lesser time, the concept of hydroponics would be best for you.

12) Stress-relieving

The era of the 21st century shows the concept of a stressful life, which shows the routine of hectic work and stressful schedule. Health experts are trying to find some solution to make life stress-free in this world of fear. According to the experts, hydroponic farming or gardening would be perfect for you as a hobby to avoid the stress from your life.

Disadvantages

1) It requires your time and significant commitment

The hydroponic system is the excellent scientific way of growing plants without soil. Though it will give better results, it is not the natural technique. That is why it requires your time and commitment.

2) Demand technical knowledge and experience

A hydroponic system is a combination of various equipment. It needs specific technical expertise and some years of experience to grow plants.

3) Organic debates

Soil-based farming or growing of plants is a natural way of producing something like plants or crops. But a huge debate is going on the topic of is hydroponic growing organic or not?

Some people are saying they are not natural because they do it have microbiomes which are present only in soil-based becoming.

4) Risk of water and electricity

Water and electricity is the deadliest combination of the world. And the hydroponic system solely works on water and electricity. So, the proximity of water and electric can cause something deadliest.

5) System failure

A hydroponic system runs or functions on the electric system. So, something error in power can create a system failure.

6) Initial expenses

The establishment of a hydroponic system, purchasing of equipment such as container or reservoir, timer, water pump, lights and water stone, various nutrients, and other things will cost you more.

7) Long return investment

Indeed, the establishment of a hydroponic system at a significant level such as for a commercial purpose will cost you more because it requires a massive initial investment and extended also. The ROI is also not sure enough because investors do not easily invest their money in a developing sector of Agri.

8) Diseases may spread rapidly

Hydroponic farming is the process of a closed system, and sometimes the plant's roots get infected by viruses and pests, and it may quickly spread all over the network.

The benefits of hydroponics

Comprehensive studies have been conducted on hydroponic gardening since Gericke. Gericke proved that plants grown in hydroponics systems will grow up to 50% faster than plants grown in soil, as well as growing bigger and healthier fruits, vegetables and herbs. Benefits are not solely related to growth. There are also environmental benefits.

Growth Benefits

No Yard Required

Nutrients

Water-Saving

Higher Yields

Affordable

Enjoyment

Year-round Growing

Relaxation

Family Experience

You do not need a yard to start your hydroponic garden. You can get it set up on a patio, small yard, or in your home, without worries. The nutrients are supplied via the water solution, so you won't have to worry about what plant food to purchase and add to the soil.

Water-saving is often the one thing that puzzles individuals. How can you save water, if you are using a water based gardening system? Think about how you water your plants that are in soil. You are not sure how much to water them or whether there is too much water in the lower layers of soil. There can also be a lot of waste, when the water runs off. With a hydroponic system everything is cycled in containers, so the water goes into the plant container, out the bottom, and into a gray water tank, where the water is then cleaned and cycled around again.

With more nutrients reaching the plant roots through the water, you have higher yields than the one or two fruits/vegetables that grow on your soil based plants.

The initial system can be set up for as little as $50 or as much as $500. It all depends on if you go with pre-made items or build your own hydroponics system. It makes it more affordable than constantly buying new plants, soil, and plant food for a soil based system.

Anyone who grows via hydroponics finds they enjoy gardening more, are relaxed, and can make it a family experience.

Designing and setting up the system can involve the entire family. Your children can enjoy picking vegetables, herbs, and fruits right from the plants when they want to eat something.

You also obtain better quality food from your hydroponic garden. It is higher quality because you do not have to worry, as much about pests. There are various ways you can ensure pests do not get into your plants.

Lastly, with a hydroponic garden, you never have to be concerned about frost and frozen ground. You are able to grow your plants indoors or move the system indoors during the colder months. With a year round yield, you get to eat your favorite fruits and veggies all the time.

Environmental Benefits of Hydroponics

Hydroponics is based on a recycling system. Not only can you recycle the materials you build your system out of, but you can also recycle the water you use. With the recycling system, you are going to use 10% less than many of the traditional hydroponic systems, and definitely 10% less than your regular soil garden.

Pesticides and herbicides that usually flow into the ground as you spray to protect your plants are unneeded with hydroponic gardens, which also benefits the earth. Since you are not dependent on the small slices are earth left with any nutrients to grow your garden, you are also helping the earth with your gardening system.

Soil Garden Benefits

Soil gardens do offer a few benefits. The first is a lower initial cost. You can start your garden with plants in the ground. However, water, fertilizer, and pesticides quickly increase the long term costs of soil gardens.

Soil gardens do not require electricity, and hydroponics gardens will. Most hydroponics gardens are set up indoors and require a proper light source. Some systems also contain electrical pumps to help aerate the water for the roots.

Soil gardening has a lower risk of bacteria and mold growth. Water gardens are moister, which some plants are susceptible to growth mold and bacteria.

Chapter 3

Different type of hydroponic systems

There are various types of hydroponic systems. In this chapter we will give an overview of the most commonly used ones

The drip system or continuous drip

One of the most popular growing systems, the drip system is an active system that can be operated in either recovery or a non-recovery way. Pumps with supply lines that go to each plant are used in this growing system. A timer-controlled and standardized method of feeding the solution through drips is connected to the supply. The pumps are the mechanism that make continuous drips possible. This method can easily be made into a recovery system by placing a tray under the plants to catch any unabsorbed solution and return it to the supply container for recirculation. However, recovery systems pose the possibility of causing the solutions effectiveness to lessen, as the reusing of it reduces its potency.

The benefit of the drip system is that it is easy to control the amount of moisture that is taken up by your plants. Consider using river rock as your growing medium if using the drip system.

Although they don't sound anything alike, the drip system shares almost the same equipment and design as with ebb and flow. This, of course, is made possible by attaching a drip line from the pump and then lining it across the medium. Gardeners can also add a drip manifold to have water drop from above.

Since the plants will not absorb every last drop of the water solution, the excesses will collect at the bottom. These need to be directed back to the reservoir, and that's why a drain pipe must still be attached.

It may sound silly and ineffective, but the drip system has its advantages over the ebb and flow. First off, it requires lesser water. Second, the water can be directed at the exact locations of the roots. Not only will this prevent the crops from drowning, but it will also save the gardener from frequent pH adjustments.

Recirculating systems are convenient in some ways, but they are the most prone to pH shifts. The higher the activity of the plant, the greater the fluctuations of the pH. Naturally, once the plant had fed on the water solution delivered by the pump, it will fall back to the reservoir with its pH already changed. And once it gets mixed with the rest of the solution, the entire liquid's pH level will change.

The ebb and flow system

The ebb-flow system, which involves a flood-and-drain concept, is another hydroponics system that is popular among many growers of hydroponics plants. It is easy to build, uses almost any accessible material, and will not cost you that much.

In the ebb-flow hydroponics system, your plant's root systems are flooded on-purpose with the nutrient solution. This flooding is done on a periodic basis, not continuously.

To build the ebb-flow system, you will need these materials: A submersible pump (pond/fountain); a tubing that will run from the reservoir (via the submersible pump) to the area to be flooded; an overflow tube set (make sure it is set to your preferred waterline), and a light timer for controlling the on/off function of the pump;

It is in the central part of your ebb-flow system that your hydroponic herb and vegetable containers are placed. A timer sets the submersible pump in motion by turning it on, and this action causes the nutrient solution or water to be pumped through tubing that goes from the reservoir to the ebb-flow system's main part.

The nutrient solution will not stop flooding the ebb-flow system until it becomes level with the overflow tube's preset height (about two inches below the growing medium's surface) and, as a result, causes your plants to get soaked.

There are two ways on how you may choose to plant your crops;

The usual method -- in separate baskets, or planting the crops all together in a tray.

The setup of the first option closely resembles the system used by the recirculating water method. The difference, however, is that the water here needs to be wholly drained right after the pumping stops.

The second option, on the other hand, will make hydroponics gardening a little easier. There will be no need to attach line after line of hose because the growing tray may sit directly above the reservoir. It will only require a tube leading to the tray, and another one where the water can drain back to the reservoir.

Since there are is a wide space to fill, the best growing medium to use here are pebbles or gravel. This will be heavy, of course, so make sure to use sturdy materials. One advantage of not limiting the space of the plants is that you can opt for crops with wider root spans. But should you really go for such crops, make sure to allow a wide enough space for each.

Collect the rest of the materials needed for the system after deciding on a planting method. Aside from the water reservoir, planting basket or tray, growing medium, air pump, and air stone, you will need a fountain pump and a timer.

With the use of the fountain pump, the goal of the system is to flood the plant baskets or tray with the solution water. Again, to keep it from overflowing and thus spilling, attach an overflow tube in the opposite end of the tray. How long the system should be flooding the tray or basket depends on the type of crops and the amount of water being pumped.

Gardeners should be careful about choosing the type of growing medium. Although pebbles and gravel are recommended, the more significant determining factor is the type of crop. If, however, the gardener does not have a wide choice, then what he would need to adjust is the frequency of watering. Pebbles and gravel keep the roots well aerated but they don't hold water. The only solution to prevent the crops from suffering is to have the pump work twice or thrice a day.

If you choose to grow your hydroponics herbs and vegetables in an ebb-flow system, keep in mind that you need to avoid using a growing medium that tend to float. Perlite and vermiculite are good examples of such growing medium.

The water culture growing system

Home gardeners and commercial, large-scale growers alike find the water culture system a truly effective way of growing plants hydroponically.

Besides being a concept that is not too difficult or too complicated to understand, the water culture system is also an extremely inexpensive hydroponics system to build. This is the reason many beginners in growing hydroponic plants at home see the water culture system as an ideal means to try their hand at soil-free gardening.

In using the water culture system, it is important to see that your growing medium does not take up too much moisture, to the point that it becomes saturated. What you are aiming for is to keep the bottom moist and the top dry – this will encourage your plants roots to grow downward and reach for the nutrient solution.

You can always use your imagination to build a water culture system using a number of different materials (you don't have to limit yourself to the ones presented right below).

This is one of the simplest forms of hydroponic growing. It is a floating garden. However, instead of floating on ordinary water, the plants are placed on Styrofoam platforms and placed in a pool of nutrient solution. Pumps are still used, not to supply plants with solutions, but to provide oxygen. In a way, it is a non-recovery method because all the nutrient solution is placed in a large container so that the plants can float on it, with no recirculation being needed. After the plants have consumed almost all of the supply, the solution can be easily replaced.

What will complicate this a little, however, is the air pump that would need to run from under the reservoir. So basically, aside from the water reservoir, plant basket, and growing medium, you would need an additional air pump, airstone, and air hose to set this up.

Again, you can opt to build this system from scrap materials. But since this will make use of electrically powered items, it's a wiser decision to buy newer or sturdier materials instead.

The ideal medium for this method are oasis cubes because before the crops can be transferred to this type of system, the plants first need to develop long enough roots. There will be nothing, after all, to deliver the water to the growing medium. And that means the roots themselves need to be submerged into the nutrient water to feed.

It turns out roots are a lot closer to fish; they pick out the dissolved oxygen (DO) in the water to breathe. But just like the nutrients, the plants will exhaust the liquid's supply of DO. Thus, it needs to be constantly replenished; otherwise, the crops will drown. The good thing about DO is that it doesn't actually take much to produce them. Other than pumping air and creating minute bubbles, there are other much simpler ways of re supplying oxygen in H_2O.

Falling water

Think of waterfalls in this method, and the churning it creates at the bottom. That's an example of nature supplying its bodies of waters with heavy loads of dissolved oxygen. Basically, any kind of disturbance made from the surface will add DO. Of course, however, lesser volumes of water and shallower agitations mean fewer DOs.

The problem with falling water is that it's better suited for large hydroponics systems. Just imagine how much effort it would require to design a series of waterfalls in your home. Besides, small crops wouldn't need that much oxygen to survive. If, however, you are planning on growing heavy feeders, like root crops, then the falling water method might work for you.

Recirculating water

This water culture method is a combination of falling water and ebb and flow, and it's more complicated than everything previously discussed. To circulate the water, a fountain pump, overflow tubes, and another series of hose need to be added to the list of materials.

Start setting this up by attaching the air pump and fountain pump to the central reservoir -- a bucket or any container without a crop feeding on top of it. Then line the buckets with the crops before the reservoir, and connect them all with the hose. These tubes will lead the excess water back to the central reservoir. And the entire process will repeat from the beginning.

Aside from the DO created by the air pump in the central reservoir, additional oxygen shall be delivered by the falling water action created by the fountain pump. Another advantage of the recirculating water method is the fact that the gardener only needs to check the water solution in the central reservoir. You wouldn't need to go over each bucket to check the pH and make adjustments.

The wick system

Another type of passive non-recovery growing system, the wick system does not use pumps and moving. A wick is attached to as many areas as needed, making the supply constant through capillary action. This is the process in which liquid travels or crawls through the medium (in this case, the wicks), towards the growing mediums. This style is not advisable for many plants because large plants that absorb large amounts of solution can use up all of the solutions that the wick provides. Because of this, smaller plants are not able to absorb the nutrients that they need.

The wick system of growing hydroponics plants does not rely on any air pumps or any special components to bring water to your plants' roots; rather, it depends on the moisture it is able to wick or take up through the fabric.

As a beginner in hydroponic gardening, the wick system may be the ideal system to work with, since there are no moving parts, pumps, or electricity for you to have to deal with.

When using the wick system in growing your hydroponics herbs and vegetables, you still have the option to use an air pump in your system's reservoir.

The wick system is a useful hydroponics system to work with for people living in areas where electricity is unreliable.

If you have kids who are interested in learning about hydroponics, you will find that the wick system is an excellent vehicle for explaining to them the process of plant growth.

Building your own hydroponics garden using the wick system only requires you to gather the following materials: A bucket to serve as the reservoir, another bucket to serve as your plant's container, a piece of wicking rope or several strips of felt fabric, and a growing media (perlite, vermiculite, and coco noir are good choices).

Working with the wick system is relatively easy. As its name implies, and with the help of some capillary action, you allow the nutrient solution that is in the reservoir to be wicked up to your plants. To put it simply, the wick system brings water to your hydroponics herbs and vegetables by sucking up water like a sponge.

This growing method is the simplest among the rest. Therefore, if you are a hesitant beginner, wanting only to explore hydroponics, then this is the best place to start. The only materials needed for the wick system are the following:

- Water container or reservoir
- Growing medium
- Wicking material
- Plant basket

There is almost no expense in setting the wick system up. Scrap home items can substitute everything listed above. The water container and plant basket, for example, can be replaced by empty water or soda bottle. Simply cut it in half, use the bottom as the reservoir, then turn the top upside down and use it as the basket.

You still have the option of buying brand new items for each listed material. Plastic bottles, after all, allow for only a single head of lettuce, or stem of herbs. If you want one reservoir to support several slots, then go for wide plastic storage containers. Drill six round holes on its lid, measuring at least 2 inches in diameter, then buy plant baskets in hydroponic stores. These baskets are about the size of yogurt cups, black in color, and slatted at the bottom and sides.

You can also use your imagination to design a different way of how the system will be put together. Just remember, however, that the system's primary function must still work in your design.

If, however, investing time and effort in creating your own from scratch is impossible, then opt for ready-made systems instead. Just like the plant basket, however, you may have to specifically visit hydroponics stores since not all gardening or horticulture shops have opened their shelves to this yet.

The logic behind this is simple. Keep in mind that the most essential function of a growing method is its delivery of the nutrient solution to the plant. And as its name suggests, the wick system wicks the water up to the growing medium. This means two things:

The wicking material must be highly effective at channeling the water upward. You can measure how much it can transport by dipping a strip of the material in a glass of water, then connecting it to a smaller container above. You will eventually have to know this because different crops need different amounts of water. By seeing how much one can wick, you'll be able to estimate how many strips or strings will be needed to supply the right amount to the growing medium.

The perfect growing medium for this system will depend on the wicking material and the crop. If the plant requires large amounts of water, or if the wicking material is not as efficient, then a medium with excellent absorption and retention qualities should be opted for. On the other hand, if the water requirements of the crop aren't that great, then a medium with balanced absorption and aeration qualities will be enough.

The aeroponic system

This is the most state-of-the-art innovation among the different hydroponic growing methods. Like in Nutrient Film Technology. It can be considered an active method because it uses pumps to mist the roots of the plants with a nutrient solution.

You will find that you may not have to use as much growing medium if you use the aeroponics system in growing your hydroponics herbs and vegetables. This type of hydroponics system allows your plant roots to be suspended in the air while being frequently misted with the nutrient solution; as a result, the roots are kept from drying out.

Using the aeroponics system requires that you plant your seeds first in starter cubes or baskets; once they get big enough, they can be transferred to the aeroponics system. The only issue you may have to deal with in using the aeroponics system is preventing the stem from rotting, which you can accomplish by keeping your growing medium from being saturated with water.

The aquaponic system

Hydroponic gardening is not organic. And only because it makes use of synthetic nutrient solutions to feed the plants. There is a way to fully make hydroponic gardening organic, and that's by modifying it to become an aquaponic system.

The first two growing methods are not entirely compatible with aquaponics, but the rest of the systems are. And basically, the only thing that needs to be added to transform them into an aquaponic systems are fish.

Basically, the fish are the substitute for nutrient solutions. Instead of mixing in synthetic solutions to feed the plants, these fish will produce the nutrients for you. Their excrement is rich in organic plant-essential minerals. When the system pumps water from the reservoir, where the fish should be, it delivers the fish excrement to the plants. And in return, the plants use them as food.

Of course, yielding truly organic fruits and vegetables will depend on the food of the fish. Cheap feed from local pet shops are equally inorganic as the nutrient solutions. Therefore, if the fish have been feeding on these, then by definition, the aquaponic system is not producing 100% organic harvests. But of course, should you feed the fishes with their natural food, like insects, fungi, plants, or other fish(depending on its breed), you will yield 100% organic fruits and vegetables.

NFT (Nutrient Film Technique) System

You will be using small starter cubes or starter baskets and just let your plant roots hang in the direction of the flowing water.

The critical thing to keep in mind when using the NFT system is to keep the starter cubes or baskets away from the water supply. This ensures that they do not become saturated, which causes your plant stems to rot.

This design is probably the most unique. First off, it makes use of PVC pipes instead of trays or large plastic storage boxes. Also, the system will be pumping water day and night; therefore, it will not require a timer. And although this is another recirculating system, it does not deliver the water solution directly to the growing medium.

In the NFT system, the crops are planted in separate baskets along the length of the pipe. The solution water is then made to flow inside thinly. There is one crucial factor determining the efficiency of this growing method; the flow rate. Have it flow too fast, and the plants may not be able to absorb water. Have too much water flow, and you put the roots at risk of getting ripped and torn off. The system has to maintain balance, and luckily for 21st-century gardeners, scientists have already provided a simple guide to make the NFT system work to your advantage.

A tube length between 30 to 40 inches requires a 1-inch drop. Therefore, if your growing tube is twice that length, then it must be sloped by 2 inches, and so on. And as for the volume of the water, a flow rate of a maximum of 2 liters per minute should be enough. Know, however, that seedlings still have tender roots, so cut the volume in half to prevent the water from creating unwanted damages.

Now that you know what

materials are needed to build a basic hydroponic system, it's time to dig deeper and know more about the different types of hydroponics systems – what you need to build them and how they work.

Wick System

What it is:

Of all the six hydroponics systems types, the wick system is considered the simplest. As a beginner in hydroponics gardening, the wick system may be the ideal system to work with, since there are no moving parts, pumps, or electricity for you to have to deal with.

When using the wick system in growing your hydroponics herbs and vegetables, you still have the option to use an air pump in your system's reservoir.

The wick system is a useful hydroponics system to work with for people living in areas where electricity is unreliable.

If you have kids who are interested in learning about hydroponics, you will find that the wick system is a good vehicle for explaining to them the process of plant growth.

What you will need:

Building your own hydroponics garden using the wick system only requires you to gather the following materials: A bucket to serve as the reservoir; another bucket to serve as your plant's container; a piece of wicking rope or several strips of felt fabric; and a growing media (perlite, vermiculite, and coco noir are good choices).

How it works:

Working with the wick system is fairly easy. As its name implies, and with the help of some capillary action, you basically just allow the nutrient solution that is in the reservoir to be wicked up to your plants. To put it simply, the wick system brings water to your hydroponics herbs and vegetables by sucking up water like a sponge.

In order to build a good wick system, you must have a minimum of two good-sized wicks to provide sufficient quantities of nutrient solution or water to your herbs and vegetables. Your plants' container should sit directly on top of the container holding the nutrient solution (reservoir); this setup allows water to travel quickly to the growing medium with your hydroponics plants.

Water Culture System

What it is:

A water culture system is another extremely simple hydroponic system you can consider to grow your herbs and vegetables. Home gardeners and commercial, large-scale growers alike find the water culture system a truly effective way of growing plants hydroponically.

Besides being a concept that is not too difficult or too complicated to understand, the water culture system is also an extremely inexpensive hydroponics system to build. This is the reason many beginners in growing hydroponics plants at home see the water culture system as an ideal means to try their hand at soil-free gardening.

You can always use your imagination to build a water culture system using a number of different materials (you don't have to limit yourself to the ones presented right below).

What you will need:

To build your water culture system, you will need cups, pots, or baskets for holding the herbs and vegetables; an air pump (aquarium); a soaker hose or air stones for creating small bubbles; an air hose or line; a container to serve as a reservoir; and some kind of growing media.

How it works:

Operating a water culture system is about making sure that your plants are suspended in their baskets, which are placed right above your nutrient solution (held by the reservoir). This is usually accomplished by fitting each plant basket into a Styrofoam that is made to float on top of the reservoir, or by sliding the plant basket into a hole cut in the reservoir's lid.

Your plants' roots hang downward from the baskets holding them. The roots grow down right into the nutrient solution in which they are continuously submerged.

There is no danger in suffocating your plants' roots from submerging them all the time in the nutrient solution. The roots are able to address their need for air and oxygen through the water's dissolved oxygen as well as the nutrient solution's air bubbles (more air bubbles means a more efficient water culture system). The air bubbles should make the water appear as though it is at a rolling boil.

Ebb-Flow System

What it is:

In the ebb-flow hydroponics system, your plant's root systems are flooded on purpose with the nutrient solution. This flooding is done on a periodic basis, not continuously.

The ebb-flow system, which involves a flood-and-drain concept, is another hydroponics system that is popular among many growers of hydroponics plants. It is easy to build, uses almost any accessible material, and will not cost you that much.

You can build an ebb-flow system just about anywhere there is available space. Whether you choose to build it indoors or outdoors, you can design it any way you want, just as long as the design is suited to the space it occupies.

What you will need:

To build the ebb-flow system, you will need these materials: A submersible pump (pond/fountain); a tubing that will run from the reservoir (via the submersible pump) to the area to be flooded; an overflow tube set (make sure it is set to your preferred water line); a light timer for controlling the on/off function of the pump; some type of growing medium; a container (reservoir) for the nutrient solution; and a container (root zone) for the roots of your herbs and vegetables to grow in.

How it works:

It is in the main part of your ebb-flow system that your hydroponics herbs' and vegetables' containers are placed. A timer sets the submersible pump in motion by turning it on, and this action causes the nutrient solution or water to be pumped through tubing that goes from the reservoir to the ebb-flow system's main part.

The nutrient solution will not stop flooding the ebb-flow system until it becomes level with the overflow tube's preset height (about two inches below the growing medium's surface) and, as a result, causes your plants' to get soaked.

As soon as the nutrient solution or water flowing into (flooding) the system has reached the height of the overflow tube, it ebbs (drains) back down in the direction of the reservoir. From the reservoir, the nutrient solution starts the ebb and flow cycle all over again.

It is actually your ebb-flow system's overflow tube that sets the height of its water level. The same overflow tube is also responsible for keeping the nutrient solution or water from spilling out of the system's surface while the pump is working. As soon as the pump is turned off, the system is drained through the pump (by siphoning down the water back to the reservoir).

Drip System

What it is:

The drip system sounds exactly like its name – you keep your herbs' and vegetables roots sufficiently moist by dripping nutrient solution on them.

Both for hydroponics gardening experts and beginners alike, the drip system is considered an extremely versatile as well as effective hydroponic system. It also doesn't hurt that it uses a concept that is easy to understand and needs only a few parts to build.

What you will need:

Building a drip system will require you to have a growing medium (to support your plants' growth as well as weight); a container (growing chamber) for your plants' roots; a container (reservoir) for holding your nutrient solution; a submersible pump (pond/fountain); tubing that runs from the submersible pump (located in the reservoir) to your plants as well as drip lines (optional); tubing (flexible or PVC) that will bring any excess nutrient solution not taken up by your plants back to the system's reservoir; a light timer for turning the pump on/off; and drip emitters (optional).

Instead of using drip emitters, you can simply poke the tubing with a heated paper clip to create tiny holes. These holes will be where the nutrient solution is going to drip out of.

How it works:

The drip system allows the nutrient solution or water in the reservoir to be pumped up to the surface of the growing media, where your herbs' and vegetables' roots are located. The nutrient solution is going to be dripped out via the tubing and onto your plants' roots.

As the nutrient solution travels down to the bottom of the plants' containers, it gets the plants' roots as well as the growing medium soaked. From the containers' bottom, the nutrient solution then finds its way through their holes, flowing down through the tubing to return to the reservoir.

It is important that you make sure that your plants' containers are at least six to eight inches above the reservoir's surface. This allows gravity to drain any extra water (nutrient solution) back to the reservoir.

Nft (Nutrient Film Technique) System

What it is:

There are plenty of NFT designs available, all of which share the same feature of an extremely shallow nutrient solution spilling down through some tubing to where the hydroponics plants' exposed roots are located. The said roots touch the surface of the nutrient solution, absorbing the nutrients they need in the process.

With its fairly simple design, it is no wonder that the nutrient film technique is widely used by many home growers of hydroponics plants. The system is more ideally suited to smaller hydroponics gardens in which various types of lettuce, baby greens, and herbs are grown.

What you need to keep in mind when using the NFT system in growing your hydroponics herbs and vegetables is that you have to find ways to getting around power outages. The way the NFT system works makes your plants especially vulnerable to any water flow interruptions, causing them to quickly wilt.

What you will need:

You only need to gather the following materials in order to build your NFT system: Starter cubes or baskets for your seedlings; a submersible pump (pond/fountain); growing medium for starting the seedlings; growing tubes (gully or channel) for holding your growing plants; tubing for carrying water (nutrient solution) from the submersible pump to the growing tubes; tubing (channels) for returning the extra nutrient solution to the reservoir; and a container (reservoir) for holding the nutrient solution.

How it works:

It is fairly easy to operate your own NFT hydroponics system. You allow the submersible pump to bring the nutrient solution out of the reservoir and into a network of smaller tubes that are connected to a larger one.

Each smaller tube then carries a thin film of the nutrient solution to every one of the plant-containing gully or channel, which then flows to the channel's other side. As the flowing nutrient solution film passes each plant, it wets their roots (located on the channel's underside).

The slightly sloping design of the channel is what makes it possible for the nutrient solution film to spill down from one side of the channel to the other.

The channels holding your hydroponics herbs and vegetables are to be suspended above the nutrient solution. You accomplish this by starting your seedlings in small starter cubes or baskets; make sure that the seedlings are placed inside the small holes located on top of the channels. The seedlings' roots will then hang down to the channel's underside and from which they will come into contact with the nutrient solution film passing by.

Any extra nutrient solution will flow out of each channel's low end and drain into another channel, ending up in the reservoir in order to be recirculated again throughout the system.

Aeroponics System

What it is:

Using the aeroponics system to grow your herbs and vegetables hydroponically lets you get away with using little growing media – or none at all. This is because aeroponics is about allowing your plants' roots to obtain the maximum amount of oxygen they need. As a result, the plants are able to grow rapidly.

Another advantage to using the aeroponics system is that it allows you to use less water compared to other types of hydroponics systems. Moreover, harvesting your herbs and vegetables is generally easier if you use the aeroponics system.

The aeroponics system is considered the most technical of the six types of hydroponics systems, although it is easy to build one on your own and get good results out of using it.

You can use many various kinds of materials in building an aeroponics system as well as create many various designs that will fit in the space you reserve for it.

What you will need:

Building the aeroponics system will require you to have access to these materials: A growing chamber (enclosed) for your plants' root systems; a container (water-tight) for the growing chamber; a container (reservoir) for the nutrient solution; a submersible pump (fountain/pond); a timer (a cycle timer will be preferable) for turning the pump on and off; mister or sprinkler heads; tubing for distributing water from the pump in the reservoir to the mister or sprinkler heads located in the system's growing chamber; and tubing for driving the excess water (nutrient solution) back into the reservoir.

How it works:

As with the other types of hydroponics systems, the aeroponics system is easy to operate. The first step involves getting your plants' roots to hang mid-air – this way, they are able to get as much oxygen as they could from the air. Ensuring that your plants' roots are getting the maximum amount of oxygen results in their faster growth rate.

Next, make sure that you are using an extremely small amount (if any) growing media to hold your plants. This will help keep all of the plants' roots exposed as they are suspended inside small baskets, or foam plugs (closed-cell) that leave their stems compressed. Make sure that there are small holes of the growing chamber's top portion; these holes are where the foam plugs or baskets are going to fit into.

As the roots of your plants hang down within the growing chamber, the mister heads will spray them with the nutrient solution at short, regular cycles. The consistent watering cycles are responsible for keeping the roots of your plants moist and well-nourished.

See to it that the roots of your plants are protected inside the growing chamber from any pests that might try to get in. You also have to make sure that besides being air-tight and light-proof, the growing chamber is also able to let in fresh, oxygen-rich air inside without spilling any water out.

Finally, you need to make sure that the nutrient solution is sprayed onto your plants' roots in a fine mist. This will allow a larger surface area of the roots to be sprayed as opposed to letting them come into contact with small streams of nutrient solution; as a result, your herbs and vegetables get to grow at a faster rate after having absorbed more nutrients as well as oxygen.

Chapter 4

Choosing the right site for your garden

Here are a few details that your garden site must and should have. Let's take a look at each of these parameters one after the other.

Humidity

In order to maintain conditions suitable for plant growth in the, it is necessary to provide a number of parameters, the first of which is humidity. In conditions of high humidity, the leaves of plants grow larger. Their maximum growth is observed at 60-80%. But it is better not to stick to the extreme numbers and set the humidity at 65-75%. Cuttings will need more moisture - up to 90%, and 60% is enough for seed germination.

During late flowering, it is best to use minimal humidity to avoid mold.

Humidity is a relative concept: there is much more water in hot air than in cold air. The used percentage humidity parameter is associated with water, which air is able to hold at a given temperature. This indicator is completely unrelated to the total water content in the air. At ten degrees and 100%, the relative humidity of water in the air will be half as much as at the same humidity, but at 20°C. This means that any increase in temperature in the room will lead to a decrease in humidity.

Accordingly, if the lighting turns off and the temperature drops, the humidity increases. So, darkening the room for the dark period of the cycle, it is worth running the hood for a few minutes to remove excess moisture. Otherwise, it will settle on the leaves in the form of dew and can serve as an environment in which pathogens multiply. If the lighting is on, the humidity drops, so do not immediately start the hood to keep CO_2 produced at night.

If the humidity has dropped below 40%, and the air outside is too dry to raise the humidity, ventilation is indispensable: you will need a household humidifier. The air outside is usually cooler than the one in the room, therefore, once inside, it heats up and loses moisture. So even if the air outside is initially humid, it is not suitable for increasing humidity in the greenhouse.

In cold weather, it is better to cover the ventilation so that the air in the room warms up. Plants produce a lot of moisture, so it is even possible to use a dehumidifier. Plants prefer stability, so sharp changes in humidity are best avoided. If the leaves are bent up, this may be due to a rapid loss of moisture, rather than an unbalanced diet, so do not rush to add corrective substances: it may be a matter of humidity.

Ventilation

Ventilation is needed, powerful and reliable, capable of updating all the air in the room in one minute. However, if the fan is too powerful, it will be difficult to ensure constant humidity. You can use an exhaust fan that can replace the air in the room in 4-6 minutes - this is enough, and the atmosphere will be stable in the room.

It is necessary to use different types of ventilation in parallel:

•	an exhaust fan mounted on an outlet in the wall under the ceiling - it will blow air from the room;

•	an outlet with an air intake located on the floor, in the opposite corner to the hood of the room, while the air intake must supply air from the basement or from the north wall of the house, it will not interfere with installing a protective net from dust and insects, if this does not interfere with the passage of air;

•	circulation fans will make the air in the room homogeneous, exclude cold or hot abnormal zones, direct them better directly to the stems, which will allow air to be removed from under the crown, making the spread of diseases and insects more difficult.

The exhaust fan is calculated simply. The volume of the room in cubic meters is multiplied by 12 (updating every five minutes - 12 times per hour). The resulting figure is an indicator of the corresponding fan. But there can be various barriers to the airflow. Thus, a carbon filter significantly reduces fan performance if air from the outside enters through the pipe, each of its elbows is an additional obstacle. Too small air intake will reduce fresh air. All these factors can be taken into account by taking a fan with a performance 25% higher than the calculated one.

Carbon dioxide

The plant feeds on sunlight while consuming the carbon dioxide needed for photosynthesis, during which the carbohydrate necessary for the plant is formed and oxygen is released. This reaction is a source of energy for metabolism and, ultimately, for all life on earth, since plants are food for all life forms, including humans.

But the plant also breathes, while oxygen is absorbed, which, when combined with a carbohydrate, releases carbon dioxide and energy. The plant breathes day and night, absorbing CO_2 for photosynthesis and releasing it when breathing. As a result, more oxygen is released than carbon dioxide, although oxygen is not released at night.

Gas exchange of the plant is carried out through the pores - stomata, which are located on the underside of the leaves. In dry, hot weather, stomata close, and the plant slows down metabolism. But even when they are wide open, water vapor vaporized by the plant interferes with the absorption of CO_2.

In the hydroponic cultivation method, the root zone has unlimited water supply, the stomata do not close, and a good supply of carbon dioxide supports the plants in continuous growth mode.

When the first plants appeared millions of years ago, the atmosphere was much more saturated with carbon dioxide than now. Perhaps that is why the mechanism of its absorption is imperfect, and additional doses of CO_2 to plants are useful. Increased carbon dioxide helps plants withstand elevated temperatures. Permanent ventilation will ensure the flow of this gas and remove excess moisture.

A piece of rather amusing advice to talk about plants has a practical basis: a person exhales quite a lot of carbon dioxide during a conversation, to which plants respond with active growth. If you want to provide the greenhouse with additional CO_2, you can use sugar with yeast or vinegar with baking soda. You can buy ready-made carbon dioxide in a bottle, although the issue of regulating the amount of gas in the room is not so simple. There are sensors that measure CO_2 and maintain its level automatically.

The optimal temperature in hydroponics

The temperature of the air is a very important external factor for the hydroponic plant culture site. This factor largely controls the speed of chemical reactions, enzymatic metabolism, and the development of plants (germination, a transformation of vegetative buds into reproductive buds).

The temperature that the farmer must maintain in his space of culture depends above all on the geographical origin of the cultivated plant. Indeed, these have special requirements in terms of temperature throughout their development: for germination, vegetative growth, floral induction.

It should be of note that metabolism is the set of chemical transformations that take place in cells or living organisms. These reactions can be divided into two:

1.) Catabolism - the process of degradation of molecules followed by the release of energy.

2.) Anabolism - brings together the synthesis reactions of macromolecules that demand energy consumption.

How to measure the temperature, what are the biological, chemical, physical processes depending on the temperature and then manage this climatic factor for optimal development of the plants?

To know the temperature in his space of culture, the horticulturist will use a thermometer. Originally, this instrument consists of a glass tube in which expends a quantity of mercury or colored alcohol. These instruments are simple and of sufficient accuracy for horticultural use. However, mercury thermometers can easily break down and spill the toxic metal into the culture space. With high temperatures, mercury vaporizes in the air and can be inhaled by people in the growing space.

Reminder: When an accident occurs with a thermometer, mercury must be collected in a cardboard box, put in an airtight plastic bag and taken to a pharmacist or specialized waste treatment center. Never use a vacuum cleaner to remove mercury from a broken thermometer. (The heat will vaporize the mercury into the atmosphere, it is not eliminated, but it is transferred from the ground to the air…).

The digital thermometers are less harmful to the environment and more convenient for the farmer. The measurement of the temperature is carried out by means of a junction diode in which circulates a constant electric field. The temperature variation of the culture space varies the dynamic resistance of the dipole. The temperature is displayed directly on a screen (LCD) and most of these instruments also indicate the minima and maxima.

Some models have an external temperature sensor (probe) that allows you to know the temperature outside and inside the shelter. This is important for heating management: the greater the difference in temperature with the outside, the more it will be necessary to heat to reach the desired temperature (setpoint temperature).

Where to place the hydroponic installation?

the best place to place a hydroponic installation is an enclosed space. A basement or a greenhouse is well suited. Also, the hydroponic system can be placed in a small room without windows or in the courtyard of a private house.

The base for the installation of the structure must be strictly even and stable so that the water and the nutrient components present in it are distributed evenly. When installing the structure outdoors, pay attention to the control of liquid evaporation and ensure reliable protection of the hydroponic installation from the wind. Installing the system on the street as a whole is an extremely inconvenient option. In addition, you will have to constantly monitor that the hydroponic installation does not cool down, and bring it into the room even with slight decreases in air temperature. In the case of assembling the system in the house, you will have to make more efforts to organize additional lighting. When choosing a suitable place, take into account personal preferences - do as you prefer.

Chapter 5

Assembling the system

For each hydroponic system, the assembling method has been explained in brief:

Wick system

Main Components: Growing container, a reservoir, growing medium and candlewick.

Assembling: To set up a hydroponic wick system, you first need a support system or a container into which your plants will be held in place. Make sure that the support system is not made from metal or any other corrosive materials. After setting up your plants inside the container, you have to take another container to be used as a reservoir, in which the nutrient solution will be kept.

After you've filled the reservoir with the nutrient solution, you need a good growing medium, which will be required to withhold the moisture of the system. Materials like perlite or coco coir should be perfect. Afterward, you have to set up the wick system, which mainly consists of materials like a candlewick, lantern wick or even simple string or rope. The wick should be placed in such a way that there is a clear connection channel running between the reservoir and the support container. The wick will transfer the nutrient solution from the reservoir to the support container, utilizing the science of absorption.

Important Tips

✓ You should always try to set up multiple wicks to make sure that your plants get a sufficient amount of nutrient solution.

✓ The water and nutrient solution level inside the reservoir should always be kept higher.

✓ Make sure that you wash your system regularly so that there is no build-up of nutrients, which can be toxic for the plants.

✓ You can set up an air pump along with an air stone to ensure that you can provide more oxygen to your plants.

Water culture system

Main Components: Storage container (which will also act as the reservoir), plant net pots, air bubbler (air pump and air stone) and grow lights.

Assembling: When it comes to the water culture system, you have to use a storage box made from plastic and is also opaque in terms of features. This container should be used as the structure to not only hold the nutrient solution but also the plants as well. The size of the box will depend upon the number of plants you want to grow. Therefore, if you're planning to grow two plants, the size should be kept at a minimum. But, if it's for six or eight plants, the size should be much bigger.

The plants should be placed inside net pots and then placed into the nutrient solution inside the container. You'll also need a bubbler as well as air hoses, which will be essential in pumping more oxygen content air into the nutrient solution. Grow lights should be used, if the process is done indoors

Important Tips

✓ Ensure that you do not clog the system by planting too many plants inside a container that has less sufficient space. The plants will not be receiving their desired share of nutrients.

✓ The process is brilliant for growing small plants like lettuce and tomatoes. Therefore, it would be wise to not use this process with large-sized plants.

✓ There should be no electricity shortages because the pump-action, which relies on electricity, will be affected.

Ebb and flow system

Main Components: Storage tray, plant pots, pump, timer, a reservoir and plumbing materials for setting up the draining channels.

Assembling: It is an inexpensive process, where you'll be needing a storage tray (made from plastic or PVC) to house the entire project for growing the plants. The plants should be kept inside their containers and then placed inside the storage unit. Since the process involves flooding the entire storage container and later draining it, you also need a pump as well as a timer.

The pump will be connected to the storage box with channels from the reservoir. The timer can be set to every half an hour, where the pump will overflow the storage container containing plants up to a certain level, which will be enough to submerge the roots of the plants. The draining nutrient solution will go back inside the reservoir to be reused again.

Important Tips

✓ You have to wash and clean the system regularly, to ensure that sufficient nutrition is supplied to your plants at all times.

✓ Since the nutrient solution is reused over time, you have to check on the solution PH levels and also its composition regularly.

✓ You can keep all the pests and insects out of the system if you can clean the system regularly.

✓ Ensure that you have electricity supply connected to the system at all times for the pump to operate.

Drip system

Main Components: Growing tray, a reservoir, a container to collect the draining nutrients, growing medium, drip channels, PVC pipes, and fittings, draining hoses, rubber grommets, barbs, air pump, air stone, and a timer.

Assembling: Drip systems have very basic principles to start with. You can either use a passive system or an active system. In a passive system, you have to creatively place your reservoir and growing tray in such a way that the earth's gravity will be enough to make the nutrient solution flow to the plants. While in an active process, you have to use a pump to transport the nutrients from the reservoir to the plants.

The reservoir, made out of PVC, is generally kept under the growing tray or container. The plants are placed inside pots with a 1:1 mixture of perlite and coco coir fibers. Each plant is provided with a separate drip channel, connected to long PVC pipes, which are then finally connected with the reservoir. The draining channel should consist of 0.5-inch hoses, which are securely fitted with barbs and grommets. One side is connected to the growing tray while the other to the drain container. The required pump (if using the recommended active process) is connected with a 24-hour timer along with an air stone, at the base of the growing container.

Important Tips

✓ Maintain the PH level and the nutrient composition of the solution in a regular fashion.

✓ If you're planning to scale up your cultivation process (add more plants), then you need to add additional powerful pumps and other plumbing materials.

✓ Since this is a non-recovery process, a lot of waste is essentially created and therefore should be cleaned regularly.

Nutrient film technique

Main Components: 4-inch PVC pipes, PVC cups for placing the plants, a reservoir, a pump, plumbing materials and growing lights (if done indoors).

Assembling: In this process, large 4-inch pipes are used to create a home-made hydroponic system. The plants are first placed inside their pots or cups and then placed into the large holes that are drilled into the pipes. The pipes are then connected to a reservoir containing the nutrient solution and also a pump for pushing the solution into the pipes.

Since the system is closed, from its front end to the back end, this process is great for using small plants. The draining water and nutrients will return to the reservoir with the draining system set up by the plumbing materials. If using indoors, you have to use grow lights.

Important Tips

✓ This process can easily be used to grow at least 20 - 40 plants altogether, without any problems.

✓ Ensure you use small-sized plants like tomatoes for growing in this hydroponic system.

✓ You should regularly maintain the nutrient composition and the PH level inside the reservoir.

✓ The electricity should be made available at times for the pump to be functional.

Aeroponics

Main Components: Five-gallon buckets of two quantities, misting nozzles, submersible pump, spray bars made from PVC and other plumbing materials.

Assembling: When it comes to beginners, the low-pressure aeroponic system is the most recommended method. Firstly, you have to take one bucket and drill a hole into its bottom where the submersible pump will be fitted. The bucket along with the pump should be inserted inside the other bucket and then the inside level should be checked for making holes in the sides of the bucket holding the pump.

The pump containing bucket will act as the growing container while the other as the reservoir containing the nutrients. The submersible pump will push the nutrients into the growing container from the reservoir placed at the bottom of the growing bucket. The nutrient solution will then go up to the top and eventually get sprayed out with the spray bars and misting nozzles. The holes that are drilled on the growing bucket's sidewalls will act as the draining holes for letting the nutrient solution go back into the reservoir bucket again.

Important Tips

✓ The misting nozzles and spray bars should be cleaned regularly to prevent them from getting clogged.

✓ Since this will be a recovery process, where nutrient solution is reused, you have to keep the PH level and nutrition composition in check.

✓ As the system relies on electricity for the pump to generate, you have to make sure that you keep a back-up generator in place, if there are any power outages.

Chapter 6

Nutrition for hydroponic plants

Now that you have the right medium set up as well as a good system that will help you to keep the plants healthy, it is time to move on to picking out the right nutrition that will work for your plants. 90 percent or more of each plant is going to be made up of a combination of nitrogen, oxygen, hydrogen and carbon. The plant will need to be able to find these elements in order to grow the way that you want it to.

Think of these elements in the same way as the nutrients that you need in your body. When you eat food, it is important to get the right amounts of carbs, protein, and fats to stay healthy. Your body will work to extract them from your food in order for you to grow properly. When it comes to plants, it is the same kind of idea. The plants will usually try and get these out of the soil, but when you are using the hydroponic system, you may have to work on the solution on your own.

Nutrients

To get started are the four main nutrients that all plants are going to need in order to grow well. These include:

Carbon—this takes up over 50 percent of the composition of your plant. Chlorophyll is the best way for your plant to get hold of this and the sugar that come from chlorophyll is important as well.

Hydrogen—this one is good for helping the roots absorb the nutrients that it needs. In most cases, you will see that the plant will get its hydrogen from the water you provide.

Oxygen—this helps the plant go through respiration so it can grow through the process of creating starches and sugars.

Nitrogen—the nitrogen is able to create chlorophyll and amino acids that help to manufacture the sugars it needs to grow.

Without these nutrients, the plant is going to have some issues with growing and producing the way that you would like. Make sure that when you create your own nutrient solution or purchase one, you are careful about getting the right amounts of these into the mixture for a happy and healthy plant.

While the macronutrients are the most important for your plant because the plant will not be able to grow at all and develop without them, it is also really important to get those micronutrients in place as well. The plant will need less of these compared to the other nutrients, but adding them into the mix will help your plant to flourish and look as amazing as you had hoped.

There are many micronutrients that you can choose for your plant, and each of the premade soils will come with different varieties. Some of the nutrients that you should consider include:

Calcium—this one is great for helping the plant create more cell walls. If there isn't enough of this in your plant, it could have a slowing down of growth.

Sulfur—this nutrient helps the plant to synthesize proteins.

Iron—this one is good for sugar creation as well as chlorophyll development.

Magnesium—this one helps with creating enzymes and chlorophyll that help keep the plant strong. If your plant doesn't get enough of this, the leaves could start to yellow.

Boron—this one works hand in hand with calcium to make more cell walls. Too little of boron in the plant diet could result in some weak stems.

Manganese—creates oxygen during the process of photosynthesis. This one can also cause yellow leaves if not properly taken into the plant.

Zinc—zinc is really important to the plant because it helps with nitrogen, chlorophyll and respiration metabolism. If your plant has smaller leaves, it is probably short on zinc.

Copper—this nutrient helps with photosynthesis, respiration, and enzyme activation. Yellow and pale leaves are common in plants that are short on this nutrient.

Making your own nutrient solution, or purchasing one that is already made, that has the right amount of these micronutrients can make all the difference in the kind of growth you get out of your plants each year. Take the time to check out your nutrient solution to ensure you are giving your plants the very best.

Nutrient solution

If you are a beginner with hydroponics, you may choose to just purchase a nutrient solution. This saves you some time and since there are so many good ones to choose, it helps you to get through the process, at least for the first year, without having to worry about having the right nutrients or other issues.

When you look at the solution, you will notice that there are percentages for NP- K on the package. These are important nutrients and you should make sure that they make up the majority of the solution. The higher concentration they are, the better this solution is for your plants. The rest of the solution is often going to be filler, although the good brands will have other micronutrients that are good for your plants.

This is not an area to skimp on when it comes to your hydroponic garden. While you may be interested in saving some money along the way, this is the main source of nutrients that your plants will get. They will not find nutrients from the soil or other locations, so you are responsible for getting the right solution to help out. Look for the best one you can find that has a lot of healthy nutrients and your plants are going to grow better than ever before.

After going through this process a few times, you may feel that it is time to take on the challenge and create some of your own solutions in the process. This is a bit trickier, but it does ensure that you are giving your plants the very best when it comes to their nutrition. You can choose to do this as a beginner, but remember it is a bit trickier and you will have to find all the ingredients on your own. If you are interested in doing this process, here are some easy formulas that can make your crops grow like crazy.

Vegetable crops

- 6 grams of Calcium Nitrate
- .46 grams of Sulfate of Potash
- 2.09 grams of Potassium Nitrate
- 1.39 grams of Monopotassium Phosphate
- .4 grams of 7 percent Fe Chelated Trace Elements
- 2.42 grams of Magnesium Sulfate

Fruit crop

- 8 grams Calcium Nitrate
- 1.70 grams Sulfate of Potash
- 2.80 grams of Potassium Nitrate
- 1.30 grams of Monopotassium Phosphate
- .40 grams trace elements
- 2/4 grams of Magnesium Sulfate

Flowering crops

- .46 grams Potassium Nitrate
- 4.10 grams Calcium Nitrate
- 1.39 grams Monopotassium Phosphate
- 1.39 grams Sulfate of Potash
- .40 grams trace elements
- 2.40 grams Magnesium Sulfate

When doing this process, consider dissolving each element one at a time. This ensures that the element is going to have the chance to dissolve completely for use. All of the formulas will need a gallon of water, so fill up a container with this amount, making the water warm, and then add each salt one at a time for the best results.

The trace elements are just as important as the rest, but you can usually get a mixture that has them all together. Make sure that you have some iron, manganese, zinc, copper, boron, and Molybdenum in the mixture to ensure that it is going to keep those plants looking nice and strong for a long time to come.

Ph importance

Another thing that you will have to watch out for when it comes to your plants is their PH level. If these numbers are too low, you could have some issues with the plants being able to flower the way that you want. On the other hand, if you have the pH too acidic, it is going to kill off the plant in the process. You may want to consider having a meter that will watch for the concentration of salts in the solution so that the pH stays pretty much the same. If the pH gets a little off, the plants are not going to grow as much as you would like.

For most plants, you will want to keep the pH around 6.0 to 6.5; going too much below or above this amount is going to make it bad for the plants. Find a good kit that you can use to check the pH on occasion to ensure that you are giving the plants the very best environment for them to grow in.

PH is the potential hydrogen-hydroxyl ion content. To make it easier, let's think about a scale where you are weighing two items. One side you have some acidic juice and on the other, you have some bread or your base. Much like the scale, when we use the pH in hydroponics it's important that the scale is weighed equally by both. Often overlooked, understanding and checking the pH level has a huge impact on the product you will grow.

Water has an equal balance of both hydrogen and hydroxyl and therefore has a neutral pH level of 7. Each level of pH in a solution multiplies as it increases. If the pH level in your solution is 4.0 then it contains ten times more acid than something where the pH level is 3.0 and so on. Based on your plants, what this means is if your pH level needs to be 6.0 to 7.0 you would have to adjust the pH level ten times more than the current level. I know it sounds complicated, but trust me, it's something that is good to know if you want to create a wonderful hydroponic system. Each type of plant will need a different pH level and it's nice to have a reference for it. Here are some of the common plant pH levels you may need to know in the future:

- CABBAGE 6.5-7.5
- CUCUMBERS 5.9-6.1
- LETTUCE 6.0-6.5
- PUMPKIN 5.1-6.6
- RADISH 6.0-7.0
- STRAWBERRIES 5.5-6.5
- TOMATOES 5.5-6.5

When you need to check or adjust your pH it is fairly simple and there are several ways to do so. Typically the best way to check your pH level is to purchase paper test strips, which have a dye and allow you to compare the color of your water with the levels they show you. The only issues with this are that often the color differences can be hard to distinguish between. Another way to check your pH levels would be to purchase a liquid pH test kit. With this test, you add a slight amount of dye to a water sample. Similar to using the test strips, this way is more accurate to read and often gives better results. Lastly, if you're a hardcore gardener, you can purchase a digital pH meter. Obviously the most accurate, they can come in big pieces of equipment or in something as small as a pen. Either way, you use an electrode to test the sample water and are given the results. Find the right supplies for what you're doing and be sure to have some on hand whenever you need to test the pH levels in your hydroponic garden.

So now you've checked the pH level but how do you adjust it? The easiest and most effective things to have on hand are phosphoric acid (to decrease your pH) and potassium hydroxide, (to increase your pH). These are relatively harmless things you can easily buy and keep on hand. If you're not comfortable using them you can buy pH adjusters at local stores where everything has been mixed and is ready to go. The only issues with these are that they often cause huge shifts in the pH level and are harder to control. Adjust the pH level in your system slowly and be sure to check it regularly, and more often, after a change has been made to be sure the pH level is doing what you want it to. Over time you will develop a system that works for you and will have no issues adjusting the pH level next time. Don't be alarmed if the pH levels go up over time this is normal just be sure to check it with some regularity.

Chapter 7

Water maintenance, garden expansion

Now that you know a bit more about how to plant your garden, it's time to go over some tips. There are a few things of note when it comes to a hydroponic garden, and these are important to learn. Taking care of your garden is what you need to do, and this chapter will give you the best tips on how to get the most out of your hydroponic garden so it will be successful.

Water maintenance

Maintaining water is one of the key factors in a hydroponic garden. You might be starting off, and giving your plants the right water, but they're not growing. However, there are a few tips that can help you with this.

If the medium is still wet, don't water. Sometimes, these hydroponic gardens take a bit more time in terms of growth. The plants might not grow as fast as you believe they should because the roots may not be absorbing the water right away. It does not mean you should stop watering or taking care of the plants. Typically, you should make sure that it is getting the right nutrients, and you should make sure that it's not getting overwatered. It is all about the combination of water and nutrients.

Ensure that the humidity is taken care of at all times. Different plants need different humidity levels, so it's important to note that some plants will need more and others will need less. Do take time to research your plants so that you're not giving them the wrong care.

If you're using chlorinated tap water in a reservoir, you should fill the reservoir or mixing bin and let the water sit for a day to help get rid of the chlorine. You should try to get rid of as much of it as possible, because the chlorine doesn't help with plant growth. It is in fact best if you avoid using tap water at all. Tap water has its own mixture of chemicals and purifications to make it safe for us to drink, but that also means it can contain too much of something a plant needs or something that can kill a plant altogether.

You should also look into getting a timer for the water pump. Usually, an all-purpose timer is one of the best for this. You should get a 15-amp timer because they last longer and it is barely a dollar more for the better timer. Also, purchasing a dial versus a digital timer is better, since the digital timer needs electricity to work. You should look for the settings that you need, and you should look to see if there is a 15-minute setting on there to help you. For the best water maintenance, you need a timer attached to the water pump. In this way you are sure your plants are getting watered at appropriate intervals, and never without water when it needs it.

Temperature also determined the amount you will need to water your plants. Hot, humid days will require more watering than cooler days. Of course, certain plants handle hot temperatures better than others, thus the finger test into the medium, which allows you to check if the medium is still wet or if more watering is needed. The one thing you do not want to do is let the roots become dry.

Make certain when considering water and temperature that you have like plants in your hydroponic system. In other words, do not put a pineapple and tomato plant on the same hydroponic watering timer because tomatoes need more water than a pineapple plant. Set your garden up so that plants that need to be watered each day, once a week, or a few times a week are on the appropriate cycle. It is a low maintenance way to ensure your plants are watered, getting proper nutrients, and growing faster than if you were using soil.

Garden expansion

When it comes to expanding your garden, there are a few things that you should know, because they are definitely important to keep in mind before you start to grow in a hydroponic garden.

Lighting

If you are growing a hydroponic garden in a place that has a somewhat outdoor setting such as a sun room, you need to ensure that the area is getting light. When you are expanding, do consider the light factors that are necessary for this. Yes, grow lights do work in many cases, and they can be helpful, but you should also have natural light as well to keep the plants thriving. You should work to have at least all of the plants near two corners of the wall, and have windows that will allow the plant to absorb the light. Ideally, try to get as many of them near the window as possible, if not grown in a greenhouse. If necessary, add more lights to ensure the proper amount of sunlight; especially, if you notice your plants are struggling to get proper lighting from windows.

Fixtures

There are various fixtures. Some of the pots are good for garden expansion. You should make sure that you get a trellis or a potting system that has multiple planters so that you can grow more. Ideally, you want to consider all sorts of planter sizes, so that some will fit into small areas and others can fit in areas with more space.

Finally, you should make sure that the plants are given enough space. It happens frequently that when you're expanding, you think you can just put more in the location and expect it to be fine. In reality, that's not going to work, and you will end up creating more problems in your garden than you expected.

What you should do instead, is trying to figure out new places that work for the plant, and also keep in mind the size of it.

You might think you have plenty of space in one planter, until you realize that the roots of one single plant have spread out. For example, carrots need to be spaced 6 to 12 inches apart and have plenty of room to grow down. If you have too many seeds in one hole, without trimming back the amount of new growth to one carrot top, there is not enough room for a full size carrot.

Remember that vegetables need approximately a foot of room for them to grow so that the roots don't crowd, but in contrast, herbs don't need a ton of growing space, which makes it work for many. You should research what plants will work for which spaces, and what works for you.

When it comes to space and planting various fruits and vegetables, there are other things to consider, such as plant compatibility. Have you ever planted vegetables in the same large box planter and had one thrive while the other died, yet the year before you could grow the one that died just fine? It comes down to compatibility. There are certain competing plants that cannot grow together in the same space. If you use the drip bucket system as outlined in previous chapters, you would want to have one bucket for each type of plant, such as one bucket of strawberries, one bucket of tomatoes, one for cucumbers, and another for a citrus tree. In this way, there is no competition. Of course, you also have to have plants on the same water pump and timer as outlined in water maintenance.

Growing medium options

You should make sure you get the correct growing medium as well for every single plant that you're maintaining. Rockwool, expanded clay aggregate, coconut fibers, and even oasis are all different materials that work better as a growing medium than others for various plants. You should take all of these into consideration for every single plant so you're getting the yield that you want without too many problems.

Ideally, when starting off and when expanding your garden, you should use a high quality medium to give yourself the best start for any new plant, or some expanding plants. Mediums like gravel, sand, peat moss, expanded clay, and composted bark will work for many of the plants.

You should also shy away from using certain vermiculite for your plants, and for a good reason. This is a substance that can be risky for not only the health of the plant, but yours as well. This substance might seem harmless, but the fibers do contain asbestos, and these are very dangerous for your respiratory health and your overall health. You should avoid using this at all costs, and do make sure that if it does contain any of this substance, it isn't used. Not all vermiculite is the same; however, if you buy cheap and you do not read the package, you may end up with some that contains asbestos. This is why you should avoid using the product at all, given that you may never be certain whether it contains asbestos or not.

Important maintenance tips

Now, when you have a garden, it's important that you make sure that it's maintained correctly. If you're not taking care of the garden, it will suffer. There are a couple of different elements to keep in mind so you can have the best, most successful garden imaginable.

Hydroponic gardens may not contain soil, but this does not mean pests cannot affect your plants. You can still find disease and pests affecting the growth of the plant, the fruit or vegetable, or the overall health of the plant. There are ways to ensure the pests and plant disease do not wreak havoc in your garden.

- Keep the environment clean: remove any dust, immediately remove cobwebs, spray around the edges of the room for bugs, but not around the hydroponic system. A clean, well maintained environment will reduce the risk of pests and disease.

- The plants and room need to be properly ventilated. Disease occurs when ventilation is weak or when air particles are introduced that can harm a plant.

- Proper temperature can also lessen the issue with disease. It will not help with pests as many also like warm temperatures. However, maintaining a plant's temperature at appropriate levels reduces the risk of certain bacteria or mold growth.

- Water, you will see this again and again. The type of water, the water maintenance, pH balance, and circulating water all determine whether a plant is healthy. Stagnant water can breed pests and disease, even things like mold. Letting water stand near the roots can create rot, which creates decay, and leads to plant death. Overwatering can also lead to blight.

You can prevent problems by choosing plants that are hardier. There are certain plants that are harder to kill for any gardener. These plants tend to have low maintenance requirements. Once you succeed with hardy plants, you can move on to the more fragile plant and attempt to grow it in your hydroponic system. As you grow your plants, you will want to monitor leaf health, stalk health, veggie or fruit health, and growth. If at any stage of the plant's development there looks like disease or pests are hurting your plant, then you can handle it accordingly.

Pruning for plant maintenance

You should also prune regularly. It was started in a previous chapter that vegetables do need it to prevent root tangling and messes, but you should make sure to prune every single plant to help with the growing environment. You should use a pair of clean scissors that are sharp, and take them to the chewed leaves or leaves that are looking like they have a disease. You should also get rid of any diseased sections and any roots that might be suffering. This will allow the plants to be fuller, and to use the emery to create more shoots and allow you to yield more crop in your hydroponic garden. You can also purchase pruning shears. You definitely want something that is sharp and that will make a quick cut. Tearing the plant leaves or stems with dull shears can lead to plant death.

Tips on lighting

If you're looking for good lights, do take a look at the various types of them. Typically, metal halide is a red spectrum lighting, which is good for plants that need a red hue wave length. In contrast, the high pressure sodium lights are a lighting system that's great for older, more mature plants to help them continue on living. LEDs are the third type of lighting that can be helpful in your hydroponic garden, but they do tend to be slightly more expensive. You will see better growth with LED lights, plus you have the ability to change the power to help control plant growth. These are the three best types of lights available for hydroponic gardens.

Adding nutrients

When it comes to adding nutrients, there are some that work better than others. For every single plant, nutrients are required, in order to get the best growth possible. There are some micronutrients and macro-nutrients that you must keep in mind and apply to your garden in order to have the best possible outcome for your plant.

The essential macro-nutrients are boron, copper, cobalt, iron, and zinc, and you should make sure that the medium has enough of those by using the proper growing measurements. Along with this, you should also take the time to make sure the pH is at the right level for the plants. It all depends on the type of plants that you have been growing.

When it comes to other macro-nutrients, there are also some that should be in trace amounts, especially since these are important for plant growth. These are typically there already, but if it's not enough, you should implement a means to have them in the nutrient solution.

- For example, nitrogen is used to help with the growth of the foliage and should be there.
- Phosphorus is needed for root growth, and if your plant blooms, it will need that.

- If your plants are prone to getting sick, you should increase the potassium to help fight off the disease and to generate a higher resistance.

- Calcium allows the plant to have new shoots and roots as well to help it grow and expand.

- Magnesium helps increase the chlorophyll for a plant and to make it produce more food. This is good for any plants that need a bit of a boost in their plant food production.

Ideally, you should keep all of these in mind and test your medium frequently so that it has the right nutrients within it. There are two popular solutions, you can consider making at home. These nutrient solutions have been around for ages.

Nutrient formula 1

1-ounce ammonium nitrate, calcium sulfate and potassium sulfate.

0.5-ounce magnesium sulfate and diammonium phosphate.

You would need a 10-gallon reservoir for these amounts.

Nutrient formula 2

1-ounce sodium nitrate, calcium nitrate, potassium sulfate.

0.5-ounce magnesium sulfate

1.5-ounces single super phosphate

Again you would require 10 gallons of water for the mixture.

To add the trace elements, you can use ½ tsp of manganese chloride and zinc sulfate, 1.25 tsp boric acid powder, 1/5 tsp copper sulfate and 2 tsp iron chelate and mix it in 1 gallon of water. You would then allow the two mixtures to combine in the reservoir. You can also spray the trace elements over the plants independently.

All of these tips will allow you to grow your plants easily and without too many issues. Growing a hydroponic garden can take work when you first start, but once you read these tips and implement them, you will definitely grow the plants that you want to, and you'll be able to be successful with your hydroponic garden endeavors no matter what they are.

Chapter 8

Plant stages

Varied Stages of a Plant in Hydroponic Systems

Primarily, there are three different stages of growth observed in plants growing in a hydroponic garden and they are:

1. The rooting stage

2. The vegetative stage

3. The flowering stage

Each of these stages is discussed below with reference to a few plants that grow well within an indoors or outdoors hydroponic system.

The rooting stage

As the name itself suggests, at this stage, the roots will start to develop. The rooting stage is not the same for all plants. Some plants take a long time to develop roots while others do so rather quickly, often within a week's time and very specific conditions of temperature and humidity need to be maintained during this stage. For example, during rooting stage of mint, which is a very good herb to grow in a hydroponic garden, it takes the only a week for the roots to appear and the plants require high humidity, around eighty-five to ninety percent (which will obviously need to be reduced to about seventy to seventy-five percent, once this phase is over).

Now, for the roots to appear in a hydroponic system, you can either sow seeds of the desired plant and have them germinate or if you wish to grow your plant from cutting, then you can use a substrate. Herbs like dill, oregano, and thyme easily develop roots from both seeds and cutting. However, to accelerate the rooting stage of these plants in a hydroponic garden, especially when you are propagating them from cuttings, it is best to use a rooting hormone along with the substrate, which can be some rock wool or peat, or any other medium that can retain the moisture. Now it is important to remember that the rooting phase does not end immediately after the roots start growing. The stage continues until the roots have developed fully.

But while the process is going on, you can transfer the plants to your hydroponic system. When you do this, remember to spray the roots with the nutrient solution (an air pump can be used to do this) or the growing roots can be kept submerged in the solution. However, make sure that you do not spray too much solution, or keep the roots submerged for too long because aeration is important as well. If proper aeration is not available, especially during the rooting stage, diseases like root rot might develop, and cause damage to the whole system.

The vegetative stage

Once the roots have been fully formed, the other parts of the plants in your hydroponic garden, like the branches and leaves, will start developing. Since the vegetative stage is the period when the plant is constantly growing, the plants will need more nutrients, especially nitrogen and potassium so that the stem and leaves develop faster. This is the stage where the plant grows laterally (as in the case of herbs like basil or chervil) or vertically (lettuce, tomatoes or other vining crops) and this is why you need to provide enough space between the different plants in your hydroponic garden. For basil plants, there should be around twelve inches of space between each plant to allow lateral growth and this will actually increase the yield. For chervil too, the same amount of space is required as the plants spread out a lot.

For the vining crops like lettuce, tomatoes, and even peppers, there needs to be enough vertical space as these plants need to be trained up to the roof of your hydroponic garden, to allow them to grow properly. During the vegetative phase, since the plants are developing more, and the conditions of temperature, humidity, light, the pH levels, and EC should be regulated according to the needs of the plants that you are growing (these conditions vary from plant to plant). Chervil, being a very delicate plant, needs a good amount of shade in summer but partial sun in winter while other herbs like rosemary, sage, and thyme need long hours of light (rosemary plants need about eleven hours of light). Temperature, pH and EC levels also vary.

Some plants like fennel grow well when the pH is between 6.4 and 6.8 and EC levels are low. For plants like mint, the EC should be maintained at 2 to 2.4 and the pH levels should be between 6 and 6.8. If you are growing oregano, then during the vegetative stage, you will have to make sure that the pH is maintained between 6.0 and 8.0, EC between 1.5 and 2.0 and the temperature is between fifty-five to seventy degrees Fahrenheit. Rosemary on the other hand, while needing a moderate humidity, requires the pH levels to be maintained between 5.5 and 7.0. It is very important to remember to maintain these conditions as failure to do so will stunt the growth of the plants.

The flowering stage

During this stage, the plants in your hydroponic garden will develop fruits or flowers. The flowering stage begins with the formation of buds and lasts till the plants are fully matured with fully formed fruits or blooming flowers and are ready for harvest. The plants will need to be misted with a solution of water and necessary nutrients and their exposure to light (sunlight or artificial light using fluorescent bulbs) will need to be checked and regulates, along with all other conditions like temperature, humidity, aeration, and pH levels.

For example, lavender plants being grown in a hydroponic system, need at least six hours of light every day along with proper ventilation (if you have an indoor hydroponic garden then you can use oscillating fans or ceiling fans) to make sure that the flowers are blooming healthily. If these conditions are maintained, then during the flowering stage, lavender blooms will be vibrant and lush. However, when you decide to harvest the flowers, make

Chapter 9

Ideal PH level for your hydroponics plants

After knowing regards to best prevention and control measures of hydroponic plants, the next thing comes talking mumbo-jumbo of PH level in the plants.

We are using PH in our everyday life science which plays an essential role in determining the acidity or alkaline nature in various things like, food, pool, hair, soil, and most crucially in Hydroponic plants.

As hydroponics is growing plants without soil, so checking the PH level before planting and after planting regularly is essential to maintain the health of the plants.

It is recommended that every hydroponic gardener should buy one PH tester so that they can check the PH level of the crops.

In Hydroponic planting, it is very crucial to maintain the right growing conditions of the plants for healthy growth. Other factors such as light, water, humidity, movement of air, space between plants are crucial but, if the plants are suffering from valuable nutrients, then there is no use of so much care.

If you want your plant's PH level will be optimal, then it is essential to know the basic chemistry of PH, which looks quite intimidating, but, you have to keep in mind.

What is Ph?

With the help of PH, you come to know about how acidic or alkaline the plant. Mainly, it is measured on a scale starting from 1 -14, and if the PH level of the plant is less than 7, then it is acidic.

Plants which are grown under hydroponic have different optimal PH level as compared to which are grown in soil. That's why gardeners need to be very careful while planting plants and checking their PH level.

Let's have a look at the below table, which shows the varied PH level of different plants: -

Fruit crop	**PH level**
Apple	5.0-6.5
Banana	5.5-6.5
Blackberry	5.5-6.5
Blueberry	4.0-5.0
Cantaloupe	6.0
Cherry	6.0-7.5

Grape	6.0-7.5
Mango	5.5-6.5
Melon	5.5-6.0
Peach	6.0-7.5
Pineapple	5.5-6.0
Plum	6.0-7.5
Raspberries	5.8-6.5
Strawberries	5.5-6.5
Watermelon	5.5-6.0

Vegetable PH range

Asparagus	6.0-7.0
Basil	5.5-6.5
Beans	6.0
Broccoli	6.0-6.5
Cabbage	6.5-7.0
Carrots	6.3
Cauliflower	6.0-7.0
Celery	6.5
Chives	6.0-7.0

Cucumber	5.5-6.5
Eggplant	5.5-6.5
Fodder	6
Garlic	6
Kale	6.0-7.5
Lettuce	5.5-6.5
Mint	6.0-7.0
Onions	6.0-6.7
Pea	6.0-7.0
Peppermint	6.0-7.0
Peppers	5.5-6.5
Potato	5.0-6.0
Pumpkin	5.5-7.5
Spinach	5.5-6.5
Squash	5.0-6.5
Tomato	5.5-6.5
Zucchini	6.0

What are the reasons by which the PH level of the plants change?

There is an end number of factors which cause the hydroponic plants to change their PH level, but the main factor is the uptake of water and nutrients by the plants. This is the reason regular monitoring of the PH level is essential.

The change in PH is quite healthy and rapid as they have to adjust themselves in a narrow range for up taking nutrients.

Why is it essential to maintain the PH level of the plants?

If in case the PH level is out of optimal range which is recommended than the plants are not be able to absorb crucial elements which are helpful in the growth of the plants.

How to test the PH level of the hydroponic plants?

As you all know the PH level of the plants is very essential in order to keep the absorption of the nutrients in the right amount. But the question comes how to check it?

There are countless options by which you can check the PH level, which starts from cheap to expensive one offering a high degree of accuracy. They are: -

   1. Paper test kit

No doubt, it is one of the most economical methods of testing the PH range of the plants. What you have to do is dip the strip into the nutrient solution, and the dye will change the color of the strip.

If you compare the PH level of the strip with the chart, you come to know how acidic or basic the solution is.

2. Liquid test

Buy a liquid test kit which is very reliable and straightforward to use and which offer the accurate result of PH level. What you can do is, add a few drops of sensitive dye drops in the small cup inclusive of the solution inside it. After that, check the color of the solution with the chart.

3. Electronic meter

This is one of the most high-tech methods of checking PH range, delivering results within minutes. On the screen of the meter, you can see the PH numbers, so there is no need to compare it to the chart.

Most of the people like PH pen as a convenient hydroponic method.

When to check the PH level of the plants?

You can check the PH level of the plants at any time of the day, but you should be regular in this. You can take the PH testing step only after mixing the nutrients with water. This is because the chemicals which are in the water, change the PH level of the water also.

In the above discussion, you come to know about the ideal Ph level of different plants, and you can check it with the help of varied methods which are very simple and offer accurate results.

As the hydroponic gardener, it is your responsibility to take care of your plants, so there is no hindrance in their overall growth. Keeping the garden PH incorrect range means your plants or crops are accessible to essential nutrients for optimal growth and excess productivity.

As the beginner of hydroponic gardening, the experts recommend that you should check the range of PH every day so that you come to know the right growth of the plants.

However, you can also improve the nutrient intake of the plants by using humic or fulvic acids. So, at last, mind that in the hydroponic system, the PH level is incredibly essential for the overall health and vitality of the crop. If it is at an incorrect range, then plants suffer from various deficiencies or can die.

Testing the Ph

- PH Drops

Maintaining a perfect PH level between 5.5 and 6.5 inside the nutrient solution is the key to a successful hydroponic system. Even if your nutrient solution is full of all the essential minerals but not in-line with the PH level, your plants will still die of malnutrition.

Nowadays, there are various electronic PH testers available in the market. The good ones cost more but even sometimes, the expensive testers can also be incorrect about the PH value. The solution to this confusion lies in the PH drops. These PH drops need not be calibrated and also do not need any kind of special care to store them as well. Even if you've bought a testing meter, it's highly suggested that you still get the PH drops too.

These PH drops can last you a very long time, as they don't quite expire. When you buy a PH drop kit, make sure to read the instructions before using it. One drop into the nutrient solution reservoir will be enough to make sure that the solution is within the permissible PH limits.

- PH Adjusters

From the earlier method of testing the PH, if you find that the level is not within the permissible limits, then it's time to maybe increase or decrease the PH level. These PH adjusters are specifically made for hydroponic systems and therefore will not work with soil-growing plants. The liquid PH adjusters are most expensive than dry ones.

Chapter 10

Water: quenching plants' thirst and oxygen

Water: quenching plants' thirst

Water is a precious commodity even in the gardens. While there are plant varieties that can survive with minimal water, most plants need sufficient water for it to survive. Even more, plants in indoor gardens that are not exposed to natural rainwater require an efficient irrigation system that will ensure water supply. In fact, in most homes with a regular-sized garden whether indoor or outdoor, water for gardening can take up a significant portion of the utilities bill.

There are many issues concerning water as far as gardening is concerned. First is the amount of water supply. Water supplies the oxygen needed by the plants to survive and to facilitate the flow of minerals from the soil to its various parts. However, too much water can make plants susceptible to rotting and diseases. Likewise, similar with the issue of potability, the quality of water used in the garden can also significantly impact the plant's health. Even the frequency and manner of watering are primary considerations.

Water Quality

Water quality is as much a critical factor in gardening as it is in other daily human activities such as cooking and drinking. Water quality generally refers to the composition of the water or the chemical and physical elements that comprise it. Water with certain mineral contents can be detrimental to the plants' health.

Hard vs. Soft Water

Hard water is water with a relatively high content of calcium and magnesium. This is the kind of water that is not advisable for use in the homes as it can cause residue build-ups on surfaces and household fixtures. Soft water, on the other hand, is water with high sodium content. This is the kind that is most advisable to be used in the homes, but never with plants. The salty residue in the soil over time can become toxic as it destroys the soil structure around the plant.

pH level

Another consideration in the use of hard and soft water is pH level, referring to the acidity or alkalinity of water. While most plants are not so sensitive to varying pH levels, water with a pH level of 6.5 – 7 is more preferred. This is why hard water, despite being more preferred over soft water, can still be detrimental to plants in the long run. The high pH level of hard water (around pH 8 – 9) can cause yellowing in plants, also called chlorosis.

Experts still prefer rainwater because it contains the least chemical components and has the right pH level for the plant. Distilled or purified and tap water are also options, albeit more expensive. With tap water also, it is wise to check the source of the water and use a filtering system for chemical deposits.

Irrigation

Water and irrigation in gardens go hand in hand. A good and efficient irrigation system can be helpful in managing water supply, especially if using rainwater or tap/purified water. An irrigation system in an indoor garden can also facilitate the proper manner and frequency of watering.

Depending on the design of the garden, two of the most common irrigation systems are the drip system and sprinkler system.

1. Drip System. By far, this is said to be the most economical way of providing irrigation to plants in an indoor garden. A pipe with holes is laid out on the ground close to the plants. The drip system allows controlled watering in a number of ways: (a) it covers only the area where the plants are being grown; (b) water flows direct to the roots and not on the leaves, which can cause rotting; and (c) it does not water the

weeds. It is also more cost-efficient especially in hotter climates where evaporation rate is high.

2. Sprinkler System. This is the next most popular irrigation system where sprinklers, often set overhead, provide the needed water supply. One can set the controls for when the sprinkler is set to go off and thus, very ideal for large gardens. However, it can be very wasteful since the direction of the water is less harder to control than with the drip system. Most of the water falls on the leaves especially with overhead sprinklers, thus, increasing the chances of fungal growth. Unlike drip system also, sprinklers tend to water the ground in between the plants, hence, promoting weed growth.

For smaller gardens or when dealing with smaller plants like sprouts and seedlings, the more traditional hand watering can help control the flow of water. Best to use a hose with a water hand or even better, your thumb to better control the flow and amount of water.

With rainwater, gardeners "harvest" rainwater by using big pails and containers to catch rainwater during heavy downpours. A lid is used to prevent evaporation.

Watering Plants

The rule of thumb when it comes how often plants should be watered is once a week. Caution that too much watering can drown the plant or cause rotting. Experts also advise that it is best to water when the soil is moist so that absorption is easier as well as save on supply. As for the perfect time for watering, mornings are recommended over evenings since evaporation rate is slower at night, increasing the chances of molds and fungi developing on the leaves.

Other considerations in the frequency of watering include the type of soil, the atmospheric climate/weather, the type and variety of plant, and the amount of sunlight filling the indoor garden. For example, clay type soils absorb water easily and retain water for much longer, so watering may be minimal. Bromeliads require less water than orchids and other ornamental plants.

Like most living creatures, plants need water to survive. The need for water in the gardens depends on a number of factors, both environmental like the soil type and external, such as the plant variety being grown. Water quality, in addition to the amount of water supplied, is an important factor in maintaining healthy plants. Because water is also an important and scarce resource, an efficient system for managing the supply of water should be in place

Oxygen is needed to grow healthy vegetables:

As I mentioned earlier, Rockwool will hold both air and water, and the air will stimulate baby plants to grow faster.

Pumping the water nutrient solution to the highest point of the hydroponic system is going to create some air bubbles. The volume of water coming from the end of the pump hose also makes splashes inside the 4" PVC pipe. Additionally, as the water falls from the upper to lower pipes (or draining pipes) extra air bubbles are created, increasing the amount of oxygen to the roots downstream in the hydroponic system.

If you do not have the space to fit the 10' long pipes, you can cut them in half, or if you do not want 4 levels of piping, you can have just 2 levels. But what you cannot change is the vertical distance between pipes, the diameter of the pipes, or the drains, because it will affect the rate and volume of the flowing water, and oxygenation of the water.

There are experiments out there where people use air pumps to supply oxygen to the reservoir hydroponic tank. I don't use this application in my hydroponic, but if you feel that your organic plants need more oxygen, it doesn't hurt to add a 12 volt DC air pump to the reservoir. Then connect the air pump to your solar panel to aerate your reservoir tank.

Chapter 11

Greenhouse operation

Hydroponic cultivation in a greenhouse has the added benefit that the nutrient solution is not dissolved by rain. Though greenhouses are usually used to retain plants warmer than the environment, they can also be used to regulate other environmental aspects.

The covering reduces the amount of heat loss caused by wind convective cooling and reflects any longwave radiation emitted by the crop and air (depends entirely on the cover material).

Subsequently, when the sun is above the horizon, temperatures accumulate with heat being transmitted to the soil, thereby significantly improving plant growth. A greenhouse reacts very rapidly to conditions outside, such as alterations in solar radiation levels or night-time cooling temperatures. Through ventilation, most greenhouses drop within two hours of sunset to within 1 to 2 ° C of the ambient temperature.

Greenhouses fall into these categories:

- Glasshouses: they have (at least partly) glass walls; they are very efficient, long-lasting and costly.

•   Fiberglass houses: made of fiberglass sheets; cheaper, less insulated than glass houses, with a medium life expectancy.

•   Coreflute/solar sheet house: low cost, long lifetime (15 years plus) and more effective regulation of temperature than PVC or fiberglass houses

•   PVC screen (polythene houses): made of polythene plastic, typically over a metal frame (commonly a tunnel). They are quite low cost but only last a few years before they require replacement of the cover. Insulation is worse than other safety covers.

Certain devices used in rising beds for environmental control:

•   Hotbeds-Heat is generated at the bottom of a bed (box arrangement) by means of electrical heating cables, hot water or steam pipes or hot air flues. The bed must have draining outlets and be constructed from a non-rotting material (i.e. cement, stone, treated wood, etc.). Ideal dimensions are 1 m x 2 m (3 ftx 6 ft). The hotbed is packed with coarse sand or perlite extending 8-10 cm (3-4 inches) deep.

•   Cold frames—A cold frame is similar to a hotbed unless it is heated and has a glass, plastic, fiberglass or similar cover/top material. Cold frames may be placed inside a greenhouse or outside it. A simple cold frame can be erected at a really low cost and can be used to hit cutting or germinate seed (although not as efficiently as heated beds).

• Shadehouses–Use to cover young plants, usually after extracting them from the spreading area and planting them in the first tub. Shadehouses encourage plants to gradually ease out to the harsher outdoor world from their highly protected propagating area.

• Mist systems -A collection of mist-producing sprinklers that rain cuttings or seeds at scheduled intervals. We help to avoid drying out and to maintain the propagating plants in the leaf zone cold.

• Fogging systems-Fog systems are used as an option to the more conventional method of intermittent misting in order to provide a damp atmosphere for cuttings. The benefit of a fog system is that it still provides the damp atmosphere that is needed to prevent the cuttings from drying out and prevents the water droplets in mist systems that rest on the leaves. The lack of free water from the leaves results in reduced fungal problems, reduced leaching of nutrients from the leaves and improved propagation media aeration.Fluorescent light boxes- Many species of plants grow well under artificial light. Cool white fluorescent tubes are more desirable.

Environmental controls

These are used to control what happens in the area in which the plants grow. Nevertheless, the ecosystem is incredibly complicated, and the various factors interfere with each other in several ways. For example, the amount of sunlight (solar radiation) reaching the greenhouse can influence the air temperature, or if you close a greenhouse's vents or doors, you can avoid the temperature dropping, but may alter the air gases balance.

Each time one factor is manipulated, it also tends to affect a number of other factors. Greenhouse management involves taking careful account of the full consequences of every action that you take.

Environment and Plant Growth The environmental factors influencing plant growth within the greenhouse are:

- Atmospheric temperature –the air.

- Root zone temperature–plants grow in soil or hydroponic water.

- Water temperature-water used for plant irrigation.

- Light conditions–shaded, dark, full light.

Atmospheric gases–plants emit oxygen but during photosynthesis suck on carbon dioxide. During respiration, plants will take in some oxygen (convert stored foods such as glucose into energy) and discharge some carbon dioxide, but the amount of carbon dioxide in the atmosphere will soon decrease in an enclosed environment.

- Air movement –gasses blend and temperatures change.

- Atmospheric moisture -humidity.

- Root zone moisture–soil or media water levels.

Temperature control

Greenhouse temperatures can be regulated in several ways:

- During the day, the sun warms the greenhouse. This effect varies depending on the time of year, daytime and the weather conditions that day. The way in which the greenhouse is built and the materials used in building it will also affect the ability of the house to receive heat from the sun and retain the heat.

- Heaters in a house can be used to add to the heat. The heater must be able to replace heat at the same frequency at which it is lost to the outside, in order to preserve the desired temperatures.

- Vents and windows can be opened to allow cold air to flow into the greenhouse, or closed to avoid warm air from escaping.

- Shade cloth can be pulled over the building to reduce the amount of energy from sunshine transferred into the greenhouse. (Greenhouse paints such as whitewash may be applied for the same impact in spring. The type of paint used is normally one that lasts for the summer but washes off with weathering to allow warming light to penetrate in winter).

- It is possible to use coolers (blowers etc.) to lower temperatures.

- It is possible to use irrigation or misting devices to reduce the temperature.

- It is possible to use exhaust fans to warm it up.

- Water storage, or rock beds, under a glasshouse floor or benches, may bridge the gap against temperature fluctuations.

- Hotbeds used to heat root zone areas will also generally help heat the greenhouse.

- Over the top of the greenhouses at night thermal blankets can be pulled, usually by means of a small hand-operated winch to capture the heat obtained during the day.

Heat loss: An important factor in the control of temperature is heat loss through the house's walls and roof. Different material forms (e.g. glass, plastic, etc.) have varying levels of heat-retaining capacity. Heat is usually quantified in British Thermal Units (BTUs)

Heating systems

Two major types of heating systems are available:

1. Centralized heating system

This is usually a boiler or boiler that generates steam or hot water to one or more greenhouse complexes in one location. Typically, this is the most costly to build and may be more costly to run. Nonetheless, there are side benefits (e.g. steam can be used to sterilize dirt, pans, etc.). This type of system is only suitable in large kindergartens or hydroponic installations.

2. Localized heating systems

Using several individual heaters, the greenhouse usually blows hot air. Hot air is often circulated through a 30-60 cm diameter plastic tube (or sleeve), which is hanged from the roof and has holes made at calibrated intervals for the circulation of warm air.

The Professional Greenhouse

What makes these glass houses "professional" level is: (a) they are made of structural steel and/or aluminum and glass rather than wood; (b) insulated glass is sometimes used, if necessary. The higher aluminum and steel rigidity than wood allows for the use of smaller parts in the building, which increases the amount of light entering plants. Registered greenhouses are almost always built on a solid concrete foundation that allows exceptions and variances in zoning to be enforced in advance in most cases.

Many of these houses are obtainable in different widths and lengths and with a selection of trimmings such as finishing posts and roll-up shutters in aluminum.

The Do-It-Yourself Greenhouse

Think about building your own greenhouse if you're handy with a hammer and have seen anything at all. You will find other proposals on the Internet by doing an internet search for "greenhouse plans." It's a job that takes only two people a weekend to finish and that can provide you with 10 or 20 years of service when using durable materials. The zoning board may need to examine the construction on your property of any type of structure, particularly if you build on a concrete slab. If an explanation or change is required, if the zoning board disagrees, the city will notify the closest neighbors. For this purpose, you should pay your neighbors a visit and fill them in on the preparations before breaking ground.

More and more businesses are catching on to the market demand for inexpensive greenhouses in a hobby-style fashion. One of those firms also built a clever line of prefabricated full-size greenhouses that UPS will send to. They snap together in a few hours from what I've heard and outlast many of their treated counterparts in wood.

For just a little beyond the time you plan on spending, lumber, glazing, and hardware, in a fraction of the time, you can get up and grow in one of those nifty prefab houses, and never worry about rotting wood and termites to boot.

Selecting a good indoor growing space & setting up

The room has a few key characteristics to look for when finding a good area to grow indoors. The first obvious decision is to pick a room that has more than enough space to handle your growing type of operation, the more space to work with the better.

A window for ventilation purposes is one thing to look for; that will save you a lot of trouble running ventilation ducting through your building. Next, you want to try to find a space on a ground floor, so you won't get hotter temperatures as a 2nd or 3rd floor, or the usual issues of humidity that affect basements.

And a space with some sort of exposure to the water source would also be a bonus. Now once you've picked your space you'd like to get it all set to expand your hydroponic coming in. You can start by giving a good cleaning of the room from top to bottom. The next thing you wish to do is set up your aeration. All of that depends on the place. The conventional way is to have 6 centimeters to 12 centimeters of ventilation in the vicinity of your source of light and another in the vicinity of the building for incoming fresh air. I recommend that some ducting fans be installed too, one for incoming air and one for outgoing.

Or you have a window that you can do by actually letting it open when the weather is nice outside, it's called a passive ventilation system. So you always want to have at least one rotating fan throughout the room for the correct circulation of air.

Chapter 12

Extra: other important aspects of a hydroponics system

Learning about hydroponics systems, building materials, and growing media ... done. You can now move on to knowing about the other equally important aspects of growing your hydroponics herbs and vegetables.

Water level

Your hydroponic system's water level depends on what type of system and growing medium you are using to grow your herbs and vegetables. In all types of hydroponics system, the objective is to maintain the roots' moist state without making them too wet that your plants' roots will tend to rot. Meanwhile, the type of growing media also plays an important role in determining the proper water level in your hydroponics garden – some types of growing media are better at absorbing and retaining moisture compared to others.

1. Wick system: The one thing you have to watch out for with regards to a wick system's water level is that the wick should be constantly submerged in nutrient solution. Through a wicking mechanism, your plants will take up the moisture that is

brought to their growing containers. With this setup, there really is no way for the water to build up and then get the rowing medium soaked.

But it still helps to control the level of moisture in the growing medium. You can choose to change the size as well as the number of wicks you use in the system, and you can pick coco coir (fiber or chips) as your growing medium of choice.

2. Water culture system: If using a water culture system to grow your herbs and vegetables hydroponically, you should remember that although their roots need to remain submerged all the time, this does not refer to the entire portions of the roots.

This is why starter cubes or baskets are so useful in a water culture system – they help get only certain portions of your plants' roots in constant contact with the water. Just make sure that the cubes or baskets are positioned in a way that keeps the growing medium always slightly moist and not saturated.

It also helps to have an adequate amount of air bubbles going in the nutrient solution. As the air bubbles splash after breaking the water surface, tiny water droplets are sprayed on the cubes' or baskets' bottom portions. Making sure that there is always enough air bubbles going will help keep the growing medium moist without having to touch the water.

In a water culture system, the air bubbles generated by the submersible pump and air stones provide the oxygen that your plants' roots need. As the fresh air bubbles rise to the surface of the water, they inevitable pass through – and make direct contact with – the roots. This way, the roots are moistened without the risk of suffocating. And while the air bubbles are rising to the surface, their oxygen molecules get transferred to the water; this dissolved oxygen is absorbed by your plants' roots as well.

3. Ebb-flow system: Because the containers holding your herbs and vegetables are periodically flooded by the water in an ebb-flow hydroponics system, it helps to make sure that the water level is kept at two inches beneath the surface of the growing medium whenever flooding occurs.

In case you are using Rockwool as your plants' growing medium, you might keep the water level lower than two inches, since Rockwool tends to become easily saturated. To prevent your plants' stems from rotting, keep the growing medium's surface almost dry and the root zone moist.

4. Drip system: You don't need to concern yourself with the water level in your hydroponics system if you are using one that works with the dripping mechanism. Since the nutrient solution is made to trickle down on purpose – from the growing medium's surface to the plant container's bottom – before returning to the reservoir, the water has no chance of

pooling inside the container. The growing medium is just kept moist as the nutrient solution drips down.

You need to address the problem of possible clogging of your system's drain lines, however. Depending on how you designed and built your drip system, some water can still end up either collecting in your plant containers' bottom sided or overflowing due to lack of sufficient drainage. To prevent any major problems, always check your system's drain lines for any clogged roots. You can then simply quickly disconnect the clogged roots from the container and just cut off the problem parts.

5. NFT (nutrient film technique) system: The water level in a hydroponics garden that uses the NFT system depends on a number of factors, including the type of plants you are growing, the amount of growing medium you are using, and the way you build the system. You won't have any problems if enough moisture is taken up by your plants' roots so that the growing medium is kept slightly moist.

However, if the growing medium does become saturated, you have to see to it that the water flowing through the system's tube is reduced. Otherwise, you can tilt the tube so that the water can flow at a faster rate. You may also find a way to prevent the roots from blocking the system's water flow.

You really won't have any problem with the growing media becoming saturated by an inch of water collecting in the bottom of your plants' containers, as long as the containers are all deep enough. You can also try adding several inches of river rock at the bottom of each growing container to help in drainage as well as protecting the growing medium from being in direct contact with the water.

6. Aeroponics: In the aeroponics system, your plants' roots are always hanging in mid-air instead of being submerged in the water, and this is the reason determining the water level for your system is not an issue at all. What is important is that you frequently water your plants' roots at proper times to avoid the risk of drying out.

Lighting

Artificial lighting is a necessity if weather conditions, space issues, and other problems keep you from growing your herbs and vegetables with the aid of natural sunlight. It can be challenging for a beginner like you to figure out what lights to use in your hydroponics garden, but the following tips should help simplify things.

1. Calculate properly. A regular outdoor garden needs about four to six hours of direct sunlight each day, with an additional ten hours minimum of indirect sunlight. In hydroponics gardening, your primary goal is to mimic this with the aid of artificial lights.

Design your hydroponics system in such a way that you allow it to receive a minimum of fourteen to sixteen hours of artificial bright light and ten to twelve hours of complete darkness on a daily basis. It is extremely important that your hydroponics plants are exposed to darkness as well; they need this in order to rest as well as carry on their metabolic processes.

2. Use a timer. It would be easier for you to follow a regular lighting schedule with the help of an electric timer (automatic). Having a timer is especially important if you are growing different types of herbs and vegetables at the same time.

Know that certain plants grow better when exposed to bright light for shorter or longer periods. This makes it necessary for you to come up with a custom lighting schedule. Get a timer to give yourself the freedom to alter your lighting schedule to fit your evolving hydroponics garden's needs.

3. Choose the right lighting bulb.

Fluorescent lights: Fluorescent lights are an affordable artificial lighting option for growing your plants hydroponically. They do not use as much electricity as other types of artificial lighting systems (like high-density lights), and they provide a cool lighting operation.

You will find that you will get great results if you position your fluorescent lights near your herbs and vegetables, especially if you make sure to corral light in your hydroponics system with the use of reflective materials. The fact that fluorescent lights do not put out that much heat makes these lights an effective means of warming your grow spaces.

HID (high intensity discharge) lights: If you are looking for an effective way of quickly producing more hydroponics herbs and vegetables, then HID lights may be your best bet. Just make sure that you can fit these lights to your grow space – their sizes range from 250- to 1000-watt. It is important that you use the right-sized HID in your hydroponics garden. You might try using big amounts of reflective material, but if the HID lamp is too small, you will not get your desired results.

Meanwhile, using an HID lamp that is too large will only cause your grow area to become overheated, costing you a lot in electricity bills as well as replacement parts. Consider using a 400-watt HID light if your grow space measures two square meters. Better yet, ask for a recommendation from your local hydroponics gardening supplier.

LED (light emitting diode) lights: You might want to try using LED lights in your hydroponics garden. They produce less heat, don't use that much electricity, don't need to be fitted with a ballast, and tend to last about five times longer than HID lights.

Tips: Using electricity in your hydroponics system requires that you apply great care to all the electrical components involved. Plan your row space carefully so that your lights, ballasts, wires, and plug-ins are kept away from any damp areas or water to avoid setting up dangerous conditions. Also, make sure that all electrical components are safely off the ground. You might consider using circuit breakers or a fuse box to house all your wirings.

4. Test it out first. In artificially lighting your hydroponics garden, the goal is to place your light sources as near as possible to your plants without causing them to get burned. Test things out first by carefully touching the top of your herbs and vegetables with the dorsal side of your hand. A simple way of telling that the lights are too close to your plants is if the heat feels too warm on your skin.

5. Matching is important. This is particularly important if you are using HID lamps or bulbs: Make sure that they are matched in wattage and type to the ballasts you are going to use with them.

Nutrient solution temperature

The temperature of your hydroponic system's nutrient solution is obviously an extremely important aspect of hydroponics gardening that you need to closely monitor, but it is actually mostly overlooked by most gardeners. Herbs and vegetables – and all the other types of plants, for that matter – naturally grow on the ground, which naturally insulates your plants' roots against high temperatures. Once the roots are forced to get out of their comfort zones (within the soil), they inevitably become stressed.

1. You will get best results if you make sure to keep the air temperature in your hydroponics system higher than your nutrient solution temperature. Try aiming for air temperature ranges of 75 to 80 degrees Fahrenheit and nutrient solution temperature ranges of 68 degrees Fahrenheit to something lower. However, it might be best to operate your hydroponics system under 68 degrees Fahrenheit.

This way, you ensure keeping your plants' roots (as well as yourself) safe. Temperatures of 70 to 75 degrees Fahrenheit only makes your nutrient solution a good breeding ground for pathogens as well as root diseases, negating any improved growth effect of slightly higher temperatures.

2. Cooling down your reservoir as well as your nutrient solution can be done in a number of ways:

Set your hydroponics garden in an area with plenty of shade. It helps if you keep the reservoir's surface covered with aluminum foil or cardboard. This way, you get to reduce the likelihood of the reservoir being hit directly with too much light, resulting in less heat transferred through the reservoir and to the nutrient solution.

Achieve balance in your reservoir's temperature by adding cooler nutrient solution into it. This tip serves as a spot-fix solution though, not a long-term one. You can apply this tip for the occasional temperature fluctuation. You should also keep in mind that any abrupt changes in temperature can shock your plants' roots. It would be best to add your cooler nutrient solution gradually.

Reflect some of the heat being directed at your hydroponics system's reservoir by painting the latter with white (or any other light colored) paint. Simply spray-paint the reservoir and you're done.

Another effective way of cooling the nutrient solution is by upsizing your hydroponic garden's reservoir. This method has the added benefit of providing stability to your hydroponic system's temperature without having to purchase additional cooling materials. Moreover, increasing the size of your reservoir translates to a larger water volume – this also means that the pH of your nutrient solution remains more balanced.

If you are growing your hydroponics herbs and vegetables out in the yard, it would be a good idea to bury your reservoir in a hole you have dug out in the ground. The dark and cool environment underneath the soil surface is the perfect spot in which the reservoir as well as the nutrient solution could be kept cool. This method does require more effort to do, but using it means you will never have to worry about subjecting your plants' roots to danger zone temperatures.

You might also try making a swamp cooler to help keep your nutrient solution at cooler temperatures. Just blow a clip-on fan across the surface of your hydroponics system's reservoir. You will be amazed at the ease with which this method can cause your nutrient solution's temperature to drop to about 5 to 10 degrees less. The downside is that you may have to add to your nutrient solution more frequently, since the evaporative cooling effect of the swamp cooler causes water to be lost to the air.

If you want to go the easiest route, especially if you have lots of money to spare, you can always buy yourself a good old water chiller. An electric water chiller (composed of a refrigeration line, fans, and compressor coils) works similarly to an air conditioning unit that is specially designed for underwater use. Simply plug it and it's ready to operate.

Remember that keeping your nutrient solution well-circulated helps to cool it even more quickly. You could try what many expert hydroponics gardeners would do, which is to mostly rely on a water chiller run on 1.5 to 2 horsepower and then adjust the chiller's engine power as the need arises.

Chapter 13

Some problems you might encounter

Any type of garden or farm comes with its own set of problems, even hydroponic systems. In this chapter, you will learn about the most common nuisances that may exist when you are trying to grow crops in hydroponic systems and how to deal with them.

Make sure that you bookmark this chapter as it will serve as your troubleshooting guide for your first hydroponic system.

Rust-like spots on the leaves of crops

These spots can be caused by one or more of the following:

1. Sapsuckers (bugs) – take a look at the leaf tops and undersides to see if there are any bugs. The reason why spots appear on plant leaves may be due to the lack of sugar, causing leaf tissues to starve and die. These sugars are commonly contained in saps, which these bugs extract from the leaves. Some of the sapsuckers that you may encounter are thrips, aphids, and spider mites.

2. Fungus

3. Nutrient deficiency – if the root system of the plants appear to be brownish, then it is possible that your plants are suffering from nutrient deficiency. If the leaves also appear to be yellowing and the flowers fall after blooming, then it is a tell-tale sign that you need to check the nutrient solution that you are using.

4. Phytotoxicity – rust-like flaws or aberrations on the leaves can be a sign that your plants have a negative reaction to the nutrition that they are taking in.

5. Necrosis – check the EC meter on your reservoir and see if it is within range. The spots on the leaves may be an indication that the nutrient solution that you are using is too strong.

Treatment: switch nutrient solution

While there are many factors that may contribute to the formation of aberration on leaves, you will realize that it is better to take a holistic approach and change the nutrient solution that you are using in the system altogether. It may be wise to switch back to commercial-grade nutrient solutions, or mix a fresh batch but with only half or ¾ of recommended strength. You may also want to add a bit of fungicide such as Fongarid to the nutrient solution. Do not add any additives – these may be causing toxicity in the nutrient solution. Before you add the new nutrient solution in your hydroponic system, make sure that you flush the roots with pH adjusted water to remove any possibly remaining toxic compound.

Check with hydroponic solution suppliers and ask for ingredients that are suitable for combatting root disease. Keep in mind that products that are available and suitable to use for this problem depend on the growth stage of your crop.

When you have already added a fresh solution, make sure that the water temperature stays in the range of 21-23 °C. After a week, replace the batch but do not add fungicide to rule out fungal infection. After 14 days, add preventive solutions such as friendly bacteria. If you are sure that fungus and bugs are the cause of the aberrations, you may want to spray your plants with fungicides and physically remove the bugs on the plants.

Leaves are yellowing and wilting

If you notice that the plant appears to be sick and the signs are appearing from the bottom of the plant, especially during the early flowering stage, then you may be dealing with root disease. Root disease happens when:

1. The plant is suffering from major nutrient deficiencies

2. The roots are being poisoned by the nutrient solution

3. The roots are suffering from Phytophthora, Pythium, or oxygen starvation.

Treatment: Check the nutrient solution you are using

To be safe, throw out the solution that you are currently using. Use a refill that only has half of the strength that you are using and then add a fungicide. After a week, dump the solution and add the same solution, but this time, without the fungicide. After a week, throw out the solution and add friendly bacteria. From here on, make sure that your solution contains friendly bacteria to combat root disease.

Make sure that the solution that you are using is below 25 °C or within the range of 20-23 °C. If your nutrient is not aerated, make sure that it is in the future so that the roots of your crops can also receive oxygen.

If you are using tap water treated with chlorine, then it is unlikely that your nutrient solution contains Pythium, a parasite that may dwell in your water source. If you are not using any water that passes through the soil, then you can also rule out Phytophthora, or a water parasite that are often found in any water source near the ground. At this point, you are sure that the root disease is caused by oxygen starvation. If you think that your hydroponic system is not allowing the roots to have access to oxygen, then you may consider changing the system altogether.

White spots on the leaves

White spots are mainly caused by the following:

1. Mildew or fungal formation on the leaves

2.   Aphids, or tiny white bugs that appear collectively as white spots on the leaves

Treatment: Inspect the leaves with a magnifying glass and determine the cause of the spots

If you observe that the spots that you see are not due to the formation of bugs that may be feeding on the sap of your crops, then this is easily a fungi formation. Spraying fungicides is the best solution. On the other hand, if you see that the spots are aphid formations, spray commercial sap-sucking sprays such as Confidor. If your crops are already in the flowering stage, consider spraying organic-grade bug sprays instead.

Plants are too big for the system

There are many reasons that this happens. When plants grow too big for the system and you are sure that they will be able to fit in the construction that you made, this may have happened because of the following reasons:

1.   The plants were switched down too late

2.   The plants may not be ideal for indoor growth

Treatment: Know the genetics of your plants and do artificial height controls

When plants are too big for your hydroponic system, it does not mean that you have to transfer all of them to larger hydroponic system. If your plants allow you to take cuttings and then move the removed parts to another system for cloning, then this may be the solution that is ideal for your problem. You may also use nets to control plant height and help you maintain a canopy level.

At the same time, it pays to know the genetics of the crops that you want to plant before you choose to grow them. For example, plants that are genetically known to have long equatorial growths are not suitable for indoor growth while short plant varieties with early flowering capacities may be the best choice for growing.

Leaves appear as if tips are burned

When you see that the leaves of your crops look like the tips have burned or turned dark in color, it may be because:

1. The nutrient mix is too strong
2. There are salt buildups in the root system

Treatment: Take out the toxicity

When you observe these leaf burns, immediately flush the root system with pH adjusted water. Make sure that you throw out the nutrient solution that you are using and replace it with a very weak nutrient solution instead.

It is also very probable that the salt levels in your nutrient reservoir have changed. This happens when the plants take up more water and the rest of the nutrients compared to salts. The result is that the mixture left in the reservoir is too salty and consequently, toxic to your plants. You may want to calibrate your salt meter and check the amount of salts that are left in your reservoir every day to appropriately diagnose this problem. At the same time, follow the rule that your reservoir should be large enough to make sure that it still stores an adequate amount of water in the solution. That means that your tank should only be reduced by up to 20% only every cycle.

If you notice more severe leaf burning, then it is a sign that your reservoir is too small. Replace it with a bigger one immediately.

Leaves curling over

If you notice that the leaves of your plants appear to be curling over, then it is a sign that your nutrient solution has incorrect pH levels for your choice of crop. What happens here is that the plants are starving from certain nutrients, particularly Calcium. When you observe that the leaves of your plants are curling over, check the pH balance in your nutrient solution.

Leaves curling under

If you notice that the leaves of your plants behave this way, then it is very likely that you have over-fertilized your plants. If you are sure that the amount of water-soluble fertilizer is adequate for the nutrient solution that you are using, then check the pH balance of the solution and the EC meter to check if your plants are getting the right balance of nutrients.

Leaves wilting

If the leaves of your plants are wiltin Solution Temperaturee Problems You Might Encounterst-Like Spots On The Leaves Of Cropst: Switch Nutrient Solutiones Are Yellowing And Wiltingte Spots On The Leavesnts Are Too Big For The Systemves Appear As If Tips Are Burnedves Curling Overves Curling Underg, then your plants are likely suffering from excessive heat. Take note that most young plants are extremely fragile to heat exposure and may be sensitive to temperature. To check the amount of heat that your plants receive from the artificial lights that you may have installed, place a thermometer at plant height under the lights two hours after you have turned on your lamps. Check for the temperature as well three hours after you have turned off artificial lighting.

Leaves turn into purple toward end of flowering stage

There are particular plant genetics that make it normal for leaves to turn to purple towards the end of flowering. If that is not part of your crop's genetics, then it is likely that your plants are suffering from Phosphorous deficiency, as plants do take up more Phosphorous as they mature. Increasing the pH levels to 6.1 to 6.2 may fix that deficiency.

Another factor that you may want to look at is the temperature that your plants receive during nighttime. It is possible that the temperature is extremely cold when the lights are off, and that the plants are shocked because of the sudden temperature change.

Flowers rot

The most common culprit of flower rot is a fungal pathogen called Botrytis (commonly called among growers as Grey Mold). Take caution when this happens – once this pathogen grows into your crops, it may be almost impossible to contain it. If you notice this occurrence during the late flowering stage of your crop, then the solution is to pull out the crop as soon as you can. Botrytis spreads very quickly, and you may need to sacrifice some of your crops to save the rest. Also dump the remaining nutrient solution and flush the remaining crops with fresh water.

However, ensuring that your plants enjoy sufficient airflow is the best prevention against this pathogen. Also, including silica products also significantly reduces the likelihood that Botrytis will thrive in your crops in the future.

Plants turning yellow and looking sick

If this happens, check your light meters or the intervals of turning off and on of your lights. Keep in mind that when plants get excessive heat and light, it is possible for them to suffer from overheating.

If your light timers are fine and you know that your plants are getting sufficient heat and light, check on the roots of your plants. If they appear brown, then it is likely that they are suffering from potential root rot.

Flower offshoots

If your plants have flower offshoots, then it is very possible that your plants are not getting the sleep that they need because light reaches them during nighttime. Plants need 12 hours of uninterrupted sleep for them to reach their full potential. Make sure that you do not have the habit of repeatedly checking your plants during lights off and that the light timers are working correctly.

If that is not the case, the culprit behind the offshoots will be excessive heat around the plants. Make sure that the room where your hydroponic system is located cools down adequately.

Temperature around the hydroponic system is too high

High temperature is an enemy of any crop, and if you are using a hydroponic system for growing plants, it will be a bigger problem. The reason is because when the room where the system is gets too hot, the reservoir for your nutrient solution also gets hot, which may cause a number of problems for your crops. High air temperatures can cause some problems for your crops, so make sure that you do what it takes to lower the temperature in your room where your system is.

The best solution would be to make sure that your hydroponic system gets all the ventilation that it requires to maintain the required 28 °C that your plants need. If you find that your ambient room temperature at night is already at 32 °F, then you may find it difficult to lower the temperature during the day. The solution is to adapt a thermostat that will turn on exhaust fans when needed. It should be installed to monitor the temperature under the lights to monitor the temperature. If you still find the temperature still high, you may want to throw in some frozen water bottles in the nutrient solution to lower down the reservoir's temperature.

Yield is smaller than usual

If the yields of your crops appear to be smaller than usual, this may be caused by different factors. However, the first thing that you should check will be the environment of your hydroponic system.

Among the primary causes of small crop yields is the age of the lamps that you are using. If you think that you have done all it takes to make your hydroponic system work, then look back at the last time that you replaced your lamps. The reason why this matters is this: while you think that your lamps are still burning brightly, the color spectrum that it emits drops significantly. Your lamps will be maintaining its color spectrum if it burns within 20,000 hours.

For this reason, it is advisable to replace your lamps every 10 months. For many growers, they make it a point to replace their lamps every third crop.

White slime in the reservoir

If you notice that there is a growth of white-colored slime in your nutrient tank, then you are witnessing the growth of bacteria. This should not be a problem if you know that the growth is a friendly bacteria (which you can even add to your nutrient solution to combat root rot); but if not, you may opt to check for the organism that is growing in your nutrient solution. As a preventive measure, you can use hydrogen peroxide; any sterilizing material can also prevent such growth.

Chapter 14

Growing tips and tricks

What type of plants to grow

So what types of plants can you grow in one of the hydroponics systems? You are only limited by your space. You can grow vertically as well if you are a little tight on space. Some gardeners will have more difficulty with some plants compared to others but after some trial and error, hydroponics can provide you with a large variety of plants. Here are some tips on some common plant varieties that you can grow with your hydroponics system.

Tomatoes

Tomatoes are one of the most commonly grown vegetables in soil gardens and also hydroponics. They have great health benefits and you can save quite a bit as prices rise during the off season. Because tomato plants are a flowering plant, they require pollination for the best produce and growth. If possible, grow tomatoes through hydroponics outside. They should receive at least six hours of light a day. If you are unable to grow outside due to weather conditions, you can pollinate the plants yourself. Simply shake the plants every few days once they start producing flowers. This is a common practice among commercial growers.

Lettuce

You can grow lettuce very quickly in a hydroponics system. Lettuce can be great for digestion and is a great way to eat healthy and light. Lettuce is a great starting vegetable for the new hydroponic gardener. Because lettuce is heavily concentrated with water, it should be grown in a system that allows the roots to be continuously exposed to nutrient solution. The water culture system is a great option.

Cauliflower

Cauliflower is a great food to eat raw or as a substitute for heavy carbohydrate foods, such as mashed potatoes. Cauliflower can be boiled and mashed or served in a casserole or soup. Cauliflower does not need much water to grow and is susceptible to root rot. This vegetable will do best in a drip system. It should get about sixteen hours of light a day, which can be difficult if growing indoors. Make sure that you have the proper lighting system available if you want to grow cauliflower.

Strawberries

Strawberries can be difficult to grow in a soil garden because they are so close to the ground and can be attacked by pests. It is possible to grow strawberries in a hydroponics system but it does require a few extra steps. You will need to recreate the different seasons for the strawberries to know when to grow. Cut the runners from a mature plant and raise the saplings. Keep these cuttings in the perlite to keep the root area humid. Wait for the roots to appear and then dip them in a microbial mixture. Enclose the plant in a plastic cover and refrigerate it for at least four months. This will simulate the winter conditions and will let the strawberries go through their natural cycle.

Keep the saplings in the hydroponic system in a way that the roots sling into the solution. The PH level should be between 5.8 and 6.2. Once the flowers blossom, brush with a cotton swab to spread the pollen to the stamens and pistils. Wait patiently and harvest the strawberries when they are ready. While this process is involved, it can provide you with fresh strawberries any time of the year.

Herbs

Herbs are often an overlooked plant to grow in hydroponics. They thrive in this growing environment though and it is a great way to incorporate fresh herbs into your daily cooking. Herbs are best grown indoors since they require high temperatures and a lot of light. If the herbs begin to get too tall for your available space, pinch off the tops. The drip system is ideal for growing herbs and you will be able to grow several different varieties at the same time.

Solutions to hydroponic issues

If you are having difficulties with your hydroponics system here is a list of possible problem sand solutions.

Blossoming plants are losing their flowers

If your plants started flowering and are now dropping their blossoms, the most likely cause is a lack of energy from the plant. This can be corrected by adding phosphorus to the nutrient solution. Make sure that the plants are getting the correct number of day and night hours and that the temperature is being correctly monitored throughout the day.

Tomatoes growing incorrectly

If your tomatoes are growing but they have rough skin or a concerning shape, you can usually blame the temperature that you are growing your plants at. Colder temperature s can make your tomatoes toughen and develop a thick and bumpy skin. If the temperature are changing drastically between day and nighttime lighting, this deformity can be common.

Wilted and sagging lettuce

This is a simple problem to fix. Lettuce needs to grow at a cooler temperature. If the temperature is too warm, the lettuce will absolutely wilt. Keep the lettuce well lit when it is first growing and then keep the temperature cooler.

Root rot

This is a very frustrating problem for any garden, whether they use hydroponics or a traditional soil garden. This is a fungus disease that occurs when the roots are too wet for too long. Plants will eventually become too sick and will not recover if this problem is not addressed immediately. If this happens in your hydroponics system, you are probably watering the roots too much . Remember that each type of plant is different and should be watered accordingly. Apply an all-purpose fungicide and move the plant to a drier location, avoiding humidity. If done early enough, the plant will recover and be able to produce normally.

Leaves that are weak

If you start to notice that the leaves on your plants are drooping, this can be an indication of dehydration in the plant. If you system is automatic, check to make sure that all parts are working correctly and that none of the tubing is clogged. If everything is in working order, test the nutrient solution. It may be too highly concentrated for the specif plant. To correct this issue, remove the nutrient solution and flush the plants with only water. Use plain water for seven days. You can then add a new nutrient solution and continue watering as normal. You should see changes in the condition of the leaves very quickly.

Presence of insects

When growing indoors, insects are not usually a problem. But if you do start to have some issues with your plants and pests, there are a few things that you can do to get rid of them and prevent their return. Make sure that all containers are kept clean. Leaves that have fallen off of plants and left in containers are an invitation for pests. If you do find bugs in a plant, separate it form the others to avoid spreading. Many hydroponics gardeners prefer not using chemical insecticides but if the problem continues they may be forced to or they will lose their entire crop. There are organic variations of these sprays. If using a chemical insecticide, always check the directions and see how long to wait before spraying and harvesting.

Tip burn

If you notice that the tips of your plants and leaves are starting to brown, this is a clear indicator that the plants are being overfed. Flush out your growing medium and only use plain water for several days to give the plants a break. You should see a fast improvement.

Extra growing tips

-Lower the air temperature 10-15 degrees at night.

-Flush plants every three with with water that is made of ¼ strength nutrients and an enzyme such as Cannazy, Senizym or Hygrozyme.

-First watering should be in the morning when you first turn on the lights.

-Change the nutrient solution about once a week.

-Store all the nutrients in a dark and cool place, such as a pantry or closet.

-If you water temperature is below 63 degrees, consider using a heater to raise it to a more ideal number. It should not rise above 76 degrees.

-Spray your plants an hour before lighting if possible. This spray water should be lukewarm..

-Last watering should occur an hour before the lights are turned off for the night.

-Above all, have fun with your hydroponics system and growing your own fresh produce.

Chapter 15

Business tips and information about hydroponics

Market Overview

The stats and figures for last year were quite astonishing because the Global industry of hydroponics was valued at around 23.94 billion USD in 2018. And it is now expected to touch the 6.8 compound annual growth rate by 2024. Now, in terms of the largest market of hydroponics, then European countries are ruling their hegemony here. They have approx have around 47 percent of the overall industry or global market.

There is no doubt that hydroponics is the most prominent way of saving water and also an environment-friendly technology with a profitable business. Perhaps, that is why it has been widely promoted by the government and non-government organizations in the various parts of the world. And in terms of the drawback then maybe it is the high cost of the system. But numerous researches and experts are arduously working on this aspect too.

Scope of hydroponics

The process of hydroponic is way more straightforward than we have speculated. It involves the work of growing plants through water, nutrients solution in gravel, sand, without using the land or soil. Today, we have been watching the blast in population growth. Countries like China and India having a population of over a billion. And because of that, the food problem is growing day by day. Thousands of people are dying every day due to the lack of food.

The soils and land are shrinking day by day due to the development model of the world. So, in that case, the process or concept of hydroponic means growing without soil can be the perfect solution for the soil and the food problem.

Market Trends

As we have earlier discussed that, today we have been watching the boom of population. And the worst part is that 20 thousand people are adding on the list every day. Due to that, the demand for food and Security is increasing. And a continuous supply of food and significant resources to the increasing population has become a significant global threat.

The states acquire a huge part of farming land or soils on the name of development. And on the other hand, unwanted things like pests and plant diseases are creating the mess about 10 to 16 percent annually and making the condition terrible to worse.

To control the situation and for attaining sufficiency in food, the concept of hydroponic farming is the best for us. We don't know what will happen in the coming future, but right now it is the best answer for all our questions. Soilless growing technology is a space-friendly and can be done for the landless rural and urban people.

In the contemporary scenario, hydroponic technology is successfully tested on various vegetables and has the high potential to provide essential help in areas like the Middle East, where millions and billions of dollars are given to the other countries, to import the corps.

Tips for starting a hydroponic business

These are the business trends and current scenario of the hydroponic industry. And let's figure out some tips for starting a hydroponic system-

1) Planning- set a blueprint

It doesn't matter whether you want to start a restaurant or import and export business. First of all, you need to prepare your blueprint or planning to make your business a successful one. Planning is the primary step for every work because, without planning, you can't be able to execute your actions well.

So, let's figure out how much you want to spend on the hydroponic business and the overall. How many systems you want to establish, types of systems, area of business, and many more things that can help you in the future!

2) Legalize your firm or business entity

It is one of the most crucial aspects of any firm. If you want to start a business, then legalize it first so that one cannot be able to steal your ideas or brand name. And off course, if it will happen, then you will have the authority to sue them or pull that person in the courtroom for their sin.

On the other hand, legalization of the firm also generates credibility and faith in the market about the brand name. Because everyone wants to work with a credible and legal company and love to share their capital with them.

3) Taxation- make provisions

Another essential that needs to be taken is that if you want to start a hydroponic business. And if you have the legal business firm, then you must have provisions for the taxation for your respective firm.

Taxation provisions will immensely help you when you sit on a chair at the end of the financial year to count down the sheet of loss and profit. And on the other hand, taxation provisions will help you to be transparent with the governmental bodies of taxation.

4) Start- business account

It is imperative to have a separate bank account for your business firm if you are running a business entity. The different bank account will help you to make your business transactions transparent from your personal account and assist in auditing work.

We have seen many cases, and most of them have now become a great example that suggests a business owner must open a separate bank account for the business. On the other hand, it will help you to get away from many obstacles of taxation authorities.

5) Prepare your all licenses and permits in order

Hydroponic business is still new in the business world despite gaining so much popularity and capital value. And it is also related to the farming and growing that refers solely to the health of people that it requires some special permits and licenses from the governmental and non-governmental bodies.

And on the other hand, it would be better for you if you have all the legal permissions and licenses because these are the biggest reasons for facing great trouble shortly. And this can lead to permanent shut down of your business.

6) Get Insured

To get insured is one of the most important yet mainly ignored aspects of the company or firm. Insurance is not only useful for any business firm but also equally important for the owner too.

Because no one knows what will happen next? And to take precautions for the future is the greatest thing one can ever do.

You can't be sure enough about your business or your future possibilities because any misshaping in the future can lead to shutting down for your firm. So, you must get insured for any financial lows, any incident or accident, disruption, temporary pause, worker's compensation, and many more.

7) Go Digital

Digital platforms are the most significant way of promoting, branding, advertising, and selling your business. Today, if you want to survive from the heinous competition, then you need to mark your presence at the digital media such as Facebook, YouTube, Instagram, and many others.

Hydroponic business is relatively new in comparison to other pre-established companies. That is why you need to promote it well, to increase the growth as well as the sales. And now social media has become the best way to find out your potential clients because every single firm and business houses are now on social media.

Why is hydroponic business getting popularity?

1) Convenient

Indeed, you have the right equipment such as hydroponic system, lights, growing medium, nutrient solutions, cloning trays, then it would be quite an easy and convenient process for you. Though there are some aspects which seem pretty arduous, if you have little knowledge and experience about it, then it would be a great learning process for you.

2) Trendy

Yes, it is one of the most popular businesses right now in the world. The hydroponic market generated a value of 23.94 billion USD last year. So, now you can imagine how immensely popular this business industry is. On the other hand, it is effortless to do because people who didn't have any clue about the farming industry are now doing research and study on this method.

3) Efficient

The world is facing a significant threat of food inefficiency at the moment. Most of the lands are now listed on the name of dream development model, and the rest are facing the condition of inability to produce.

So, in the contemporary time, the concept of hydroponic farming is the best solution for the threat of food and farming inefficiency. Through this, we can produce crops and vegetables with the massive growth rate. And also earn some great profit. With the right use of the nutrient solution, lights, appropriate water, and temperature, we can expedite the growth.

Conclusion

So, these are essential business tips for those who want to start a hydroponic system. There are many reasons why the hydroponic method is gaining immense popularity and marching towards the biggest solution of inefficiency. So, if you want to start a business, they must consider these points.

Conclusion

Hydroponics is an economical, environmentally friendly way to grow plants and produce without soil or pesticides. The plants grow faster and produce bigger yields while being completely GMO-free, making them a lot healthier to eat.

Not only does hydroponics allow for fast, efficient, cost effective growing environments, but it is a means to grow produce where it otherwise was not able to grow. Thanks to innovative irrigation systems and the use of various growing media, places that have inadequate soil composition are able to grow fresh produce.

Hydroponics also provides a growing solution for places that have little to no space for commercial growing lands. It has even been successfully tested in space. Hydroponics is not a new concept but has come a long way since ancient times and keeps moving forward in leaps and bounds with new methods being introduced along the way.

It is not a hard concept to grasp and some methods are really easy to learn. There are ready-made kits that one can buy and assemble for each type of system. But they are all capable of being homemade with materials found around the home.

Hydroponics is a great way to teach children the joy of gardening without the mess of dirt and as the plants grow relatively quickly it holds their attention better than normal gardening does.

There are many exciting growing opportunities to be had with hydroponics and if done right, you will be rewarded with bountiful, healthy crops.

Aquaponics adds another dynamic level to the sustainable green farming in that it utilizes natural nutrients generated from a fish tank to organically nourish a media bed. In turn, the media beds offer the fish tank clean water as they filter out all the waste products and return clean water to the fish tank.

www.ingramcontent.com/pod-product-compliance
Lightning Source LLC
Chambersburg PA
CBHW071448070526
44578CB00001B/267